DISCOVER THE UNIVERSE WITHIN YOU

Through the Metaphysical Science of Astrology

Mary A. Letorney B.A., M.Ed.

Library of Congress Cataloging-in-Publication Data
Letorney, Mary - 1930 -
"Discover the Universe Within You - Through the Metaphysical Science of Astrology" by Mary Letorney
An explanation of your birth chart and birth plan through planetary cycles and house placements in astrology.
1. Astrology 2. Metaphysics
I. Letorney, Mary, 1930 - II. Title

Library of Congress Catalog Number: 2006937487
ISBN: 1-886940-96-7

Cover Art and Layout by www.enki3d.com
Book Design: Julia Degan
Book Set in: Times New Roman

Published by

PO Box 754
Huntsville, AR 72740

www.ozarkmt.com
Printed in the United States of America

Dedication

To Joseph – the gentle giant of my life – my foundation

To Cynthia – the constant voice of guidance & belief – my courage

To Marie – the sound of beauty – my inspiration

To Michael – the one who loves with ease – my comfort

To Joseph Jr – the one whose healing energy sustains – my strength

To Lucy Staiti – my perceptive and trusted friend

To Terry Porter and her wonderful group: Jody, Angela, Linda, Shelley, Jeff, Joyce, Rachel, and Sandy – who all believed in and supported the possibility of this book.

and

To all the inspiring, courageous souls for whom I have met, taught or counseled. It was a privilege to become witness to their greatness!

Special thanks to Carolyn Callahan and Dan Wenz for graphic illustrations.

TABLE OF CONTENTS

PREFACE

It has often occurred to me to write a book that encompasses many of the questions you may want to ask about this subject of Astrology – and did not know where to begin!

Since many do not have the time or direction to pursue a latent interest or budding curiosity concerning this ancient and wise study, let us explore together, what the **understanding** of astrological knowledge can do for you. My hope is to guide you into the realization of that wondrous and sacred gift given to you at birth – **Free Will!**

My first experience in studying astrology was strictly by rote memory and by faithfully following directions. In the beginning, it was a daunting task to read charts. However, as time went on, I began to understand the planetary vibrations and realized that the astrologer's task **was not to predict but to explain** the deeper meaning of this **silent language of the heavens!** I began to comprehend how everyone's personal journey is faithfully chronicled from the time, place and date of entrance onto this earth, and that the outcome of events would depend upon the

individual's awareness and **conscious use** of his or her **free will!**

A full understanding of true Astrology can present a broader, more expansive picture of life's lessons and the purpose of one's destiny! As we navigate together in search of a **deeper** understanding of this complex and wondrous subject, a great adventure awaits you! Hopefully, you will come to realize that the outcome of any situation will depend upon your **individual awareness and conscious use of your free will!**

Therefore, let us begin our travels together through the **'baby steps'** of astrological knowledge in order to understand the **importance and magic of your 'birthday'** . As the Aquarian Age begins, may you **gather a deeper understanding of yourself – your loved ones – and the difficult ones you meet in life!**

Above all, may this little book assist you in your search for light, grace and the wonderment of discovering your very own universe that lies within you!

My Journey into Astrology

My personal journey is simple! I record this only with the hope of inspiring the reader, whatever the age or inclination, to realize that this is a timeless study which can be pursued at **any age**, at **any time** – given the passion to do so.

This journey started in my late thirties. My interest in astrology was almost non-existent. It was an occasional look at the local newspaper column on Sun-signs. When I would glance at them, sometimes they seemed fairly accurate and yet, at other times, they were crazy and way off target. So, my attention was limited to scepticism.

Then a wonderful job opportunity appeared for my husband. We were faced with a difficult decision. I remember standing at the kitchen stove, preparing a meal and praying for an answer to a seemingly difficult dilemma. Suddenly, out of nowhere, a thought (or perhaps the still small voice within) suggested calling an astrologer. "Why not," I thought back.

I went to the Yellow Pages to search for one. (I do not recommend this method, for word of mouth is the best reference). I called the three astrologers listed...a sparse group in those days. The first one was too busy. The second one was not in and the third one answered with an intelligent voice. I asked a few questions and out poured an enormous amount of information, intriguing me.

I made an appointment to discuss my husband's astrological chart with the hope of finding an answer to our indecision. Not knowing what to expect, I met with the astrologer and for one and a half hours the description of my husband was absolutely clear and accurate. I was completely astonished! How was this accomplished? My seed of desire to understand, at that moment, had been firmly planted.

When I finally began my astrological search for truth and enlightenment, it was not easy! When I was able to squeeze in astrology lessons, I studied furiously. Wherever I went, my books and notes **always** came with me, a constant appendage to my side. I was in the fever pitch of discovery and wonder – always filled with questions – always searching for answers. To this very day, ever since those early years of discovery, those feelings have NEVER left me!

Why am I telling so personal a story? Perhaps it is to **encourage those** with a smattering of interest to pursue it – or to **assist someone** with a serious dilemma to search with it – or, hopefully, **to show someone** who despairs at the niche in life they find themselves that there is a way to understand and find freedom.

The amazing journey of my own wonderment of the universe within each one of us has never left me! It has enriched my life and opened my mind.

One memory stands out strongly, in this regard. It was about a year or two after I began my study of astrology. It happened when I would put my youngest child in for an afternoon nap. His bedroom was a small room, with a steep slanted ceiling that **always** made me feel so confined and earthbound.

One afternoon, as I put my son in for his nap, I looked up at that claustrophobic ceiling – **it was not there!** It was as if **my mind had opened wide**. It was as if **I could see beyond the confines of plaster and wood** – and with that feeling, **came such a glorious freedom!** I pray this little book will help **you** to discover that freedom, too!

CHAPTER ONE

OVERVIEW

ASTROLOGY- WHAT'S IT ALL ABOUT?

Astrology is a body of knowledge to be studied for the express purpose of helping you become aware of your own particular flow of energy patterns. This understanding can assist you in developing the great potential lying dormant within you.

Astrology is a highly effective tool to help you understand the special YOU that is so unique! Your traits, your tendencies and your genetic makeup are all taken into account.

Simply put, it is a massive body of knowledge that deals with the planets and their cycles. These planetary vibrations have an intimate connection to you as described through your natal, astrological chart. When your birth chart is drawn, it becomes a photograph of the time, the place and the date on which you were born. It is the time you took your first breath and were **stamped** with the vibrations of all the planets in their orbiting positions. Your natal chart becomes a picture of that very moment itself – frozen in time, with your first cry!

Perhaps now is the time to seek the understanding of your own birth plan – your own destiny/purpose – your own ups-and-downs along the bumpy road of life. Perhaps now is the time to realize your enormous God-given potential to accomplish great things, no matter how humble your beginnings or surroundings.

When you begin to "understand" yourself and your path in life – NOTHING IS IMPOSSIBLE TO OVERCOME! Nothing can undermine you, except your own self-defeating attitude – allowing yourself to become wedded to hopelessness and helplessness.

FREE WILL and CHOICE

Whenever astrology is discussed, a common reaction is that perhaps you are controlled by forces **beyond your control** – a feeling that "free will" is a phrase of meaningless chatter. Not true! Understanding yourself allows you to use your free will with intelligent action. It is your birthright as a member of the human race!

Only your submission to outside influence or your own compliance to become subjugated to another can be destructive and confining.

The real thing that controls you is you!

Have you allowed "other people" to control you?
Have you allowed "circumstances" to control you?
Have you allowed your own "fears and misplaced emotions" to control you?

Yes, there is the reality of planetary cycles – the unusual movement of the planets as they encircle the Sun. Their relationship to you is **very** real. Once you are stamped with that individual pattern of the electromagnetic vibrations of your planets at birth – you will become sensitive to that pattern for the rest of your life!

How you deal with that pattern is where your free will comes in.

You have choices in life!

Astrological information is not a subject to enslave you. Most everyone is aware of the sign their SUN was in at birth (common knowledge today). The suavely phrased sentences on each Sun-Sign are usually found in the daily horoscope columns, printed everywhere (from daily newspapers, to slick magazines). They leave much to be desired in the way of solid information. This can give rise to ignorance, fear and misunderstanding of the importance of your Sun-Sign. It can give rise to the belief that if you are unhappy, then astrologically, you were born under an "unlucky star". This continually feeds the rumor mill that the fault lies in the "stars" – that you are a hapless victim of a cruel fate.

"The fault, dear Brutus, lies not within our stars, but within ourselves, that we are underlings..."

Julius Caesar by William Shakespeare

Shakespeare understood! An "underling" is one who is subordinate to another – a servant, a lackey or one of lower rank. Please remember, your own "underling" feelings will dominate if you allow **others** to dominate your life or your thoughts. Take responsibility for ALL your thoughts and actions! The fulfillment of your life lies in your decision making power and the wisdom of accepting life's lessons! All too many people are willing to blame anything, including the stars they were born under. Help yourself grow in wisdom! Only you can do that!

An understanding of your birth chart can actually help free you to use your free will in making decisions. If you did not have the ability to think, compare, analyze or weigh facts, then life would be a "prison". The timing of the planetary cycles are predictable. As your understanding grows, it will allow you to consider the "practical" ways to alleviate a stressful period coming or to accelerate a wonderful time for opportunity.

Actually, astrological knowledge is a great "free will" opportunity for you to see the "big picture". I look upon it as the metaphysical science of timing! Its value is to assist you to seek the future course of action with reasonable and clear judgment. This astrological information does NOT tell you what to do. Your cycles must be explained and understood by a competent astrologer.

Then, YOU make the judgement call!

Today, the Aquarian Age has finally arrived! The consciousness of man is finally awakening! It brings with it a greater freedom of thinking and a stronger awareness of the need for brotherhood. There is a defined growing tolerance for all races, all creeds and the many different ways of life. You now live in a world that is more open to dedicating a real effort to help and heal the human race!

These planetary cycles are guiding signals, the "stop and go" lights you encounter at every crossroad. Once you become aware of them, you will realize and understand that you have choices. Planetary cycles are impersonal! They are transmitting patterns that can help you be aware of various situations or opportunities. They can help to open your heart – your mind – your very soul memory to the abundance of Life and the vastness of Love.

Nothing and no one should ever harm your expression of freedom and your "free will" choices. Astrological knowledge, when properly understood, is one of the finest tools for self-understanding!

★ It can aid in unlocking those cobwebbed attic rooms of your past emotions.

★ It can assist in cleansing the dark corners of your mind.

★ It is most valuable for **understanding yourself** – and helping to ease the memories of anguish, pain and misunderstanding!

YOU HAVE FREE WILL!
YOU HAVE CHOICES!

A word of caution here! When consulting an astrologer or any other type of consultant – in any field – accept only positive and constructive information. If you are not careful, you may be allowing your magnificent free will to be limited or crippled by poor suggestion or outright predictive instruction. Beware of those who tell you what to do, or seek to control your actions and decisions. Do not allow yourself to be manipulated by fear or superstition. Too often, only the carcasses of dead hopes survive when your situations or opportunities are not properly explained.

The purpose of this book is to help you fully understand yourself – to see your life with a clearer view – to better recognize your strengths and weaknesses. Remember, you are not doomed to these weaknesses, only prone to them!

Your FREE WILL, as your understanding of yourself grows and "frees" you accordingly, is what will make the difference in a world that seems to conspire at ever turn, to rob you of your greatest ability – to WILL FREELY! Where does it all begin? It begins with the magic of your day, time and place of birth – your birthday! Therefore, let us proceed to try to help you understand your life and to treasure your abilities!

WHY THE NEED TO UNDERSTAND

The wonderful, special individual you are is sometimes very hard for you to **see** and appreciate. You are sometimes so close to your inadequacies, they can blind you to the reality of your goodness and who you really are.

Many times, you do become so critical of situations around you and so dissatisfied with other people's behavior. Many times, you find fault with international events beyond your influence, or when witnessing your own inadequacies, tend to magnify them with fault-finding persistence. During these periods, you must be careful not to let situations or feelings grow out of proportion because of this personal lack of objectivity or impatience with yourself. Young people, especially have this problem, and, of course, older people who never GREW into their own sense of self-worth and self-confidence.

Self worth is that reverence for the special "greatness" within you.

Self-confidence is that rare and wonderful quality of believing in oneself.

Watch the impossible goals you may have set for yourself, pressured subconsciously by seductive advertising or the latest Hollywood trend. Dissatisfaction and lack of self confidence can begin to eat away at the very essence of your value system. Indeed, these times warrant strong, optimistic individuals who refuse to be pressured by the commercial thought-forms constantly generating pleasure-seeking goals and by the continual facing of your own dissatisfaction! Astrological knowledge can be very valuable in assisting you to "balance out" with common sense. It becomes one of the greatest tools you can possess to help you understand yourself in the process of living in the "now"!

★When you finally begin to understand your own personal birth chart – when you finally learn to see yourself, honestly and openly with a clear understanding of your weaknesses as points to work on, not despise – then surely you will grow in wisdom and charitable feeling!

★When you begin to develop a tolerance for your own inadequacies and patiently grope toward the realities of adjusting and loving yourself in the world around you – then surely you will grow in wisdom and charitable feeling!

★When you realize what a precious part of humanity you are – then surely you will grow in wisdom and charitable feeling!

However, before you can get to that point, it is helpful to understand how you think, what moves you to react as you do, and how your particular emotional warning system is constructed. Both the influences of heredity and environment are involved here, as well as understanding your natal birth chart.

Think how much happier you can be once you glimpse into that mysterious "you" that needs to be so patiently understood. Self confidence and self-respect can only come with each experience and with the amazing wonder of your own capacities and potential. You cannot purchase them! No one can give them to you! To learn to love yourself, not egotistically, but with awe and respect, is vital to your innate sense of worth and dignity.

This massive body of astrological knowledge, once put into proper perspective, is a TOOL (not a crutch to lean on – not information to control you). It is a valuable tool to better understand yourself. Once you are patient with your inadequacies, the confidence and the joy of life will radiate throughout your intricate nature like the warming power of the Sun's energizing rays.

So, dear friends –

★ Treasure your body functions!

★ Marvel at the intricate miles of blood vessels and nerve endings!

★ Appreciate your soaring emotional capacity to respond to human need!

★ Value your unique mental ability for logical thought!

★ Cherish the spiritual part of you that touches, in inspired moments, the cosmic level of Universal energy – lifting you beyond the emptiness of material life and into the profound understanding of that greater vision of service to humanity!

★ Only then can you learn to appreciate the great "you".

★ Only then, will your confidence shine with crystal clarity!

This vast, sacred science can greatly assist you in your quest for self-awareness. This vast body of knowledge can produce another valid method of explaining your traits, tendencies and magnificent potential.

Understanding yourself is the beginning of the long and productive road to true self confidence and inner self-worth. When fears and confusion are laid aside, reason frees you to be the "real you". You will be surprised how much happier you can be. Is that not enough reason to want to understand a subject that promises to be such a tool for enlightenment?

UNDERSTANDING

This word understanding is used many times throughout this book. Actually, that is what the sacred science of astrology is all about – understanding the wonderful, creative, spiritual Universe within you!

Therefore, let us realize:

★ One who truly understands has an endless pool of compassion and patience – allowing the floodgate of healing to pour forth.

★ One who truly understands has deepening humility – allowing the merciful stretching of mind and spirit to others.

★ One who truly understands walks the world with childlike wonder – allowing an open kinship with all creation.

★ One who truly understands realizes the being of non-being – and allows the giving and forgiving with gentle manner and kind touch.

"The quality of mercy is not strained. It droppeth as the gentle rain from the heaven upon the place beneath…it is twice blessed… it blesseth him who gives and him who receives. T'is the mightiest in the mightiest" .

The Merchant of Venice by William Shakespeare

Understanding, mercy, compassion, forgiveness – these are the magnificent qualities of the Piscean Age. The Christ was the great teacher, the Avatar of that Age, whose endless gift to humanity was to teach those very qualities filled with understanding!

The promise of the Aquarian Age is now beginning. It is the promised Age that can bring us into a deeper awareness of each other – for each other. It is the spiritual cognition that we **can** lift this earthly yoke of oppression and the **constant** REPEATING of life's difficulties and misunderstandings.

Why are we, continually, on this wheel of life and rebirth? Why are there the repeating situations, alliances and difficult emotional journeys? Why – why – why?

Have you ever asked these questions during the dark night of the soul?

Have you ever asked these questions through the fog of pain and misunderstanding?

Have you ever asked these questions when riddled with fears, impatient, misplaced alliances?

Studying and understanding the great metaphysical science of astrology has helped many gain a broader perspective on life.

It has helped free them from the clouded muddle of their lives. It has helped rid them of the fear of death. Hopefully, you, too will find out how and why it is possible to accomplish this.

We are very aware that some of you may have had horrendous situations befall you. Pain and suffering were felt due to the cruel and inhuman treatment of others, or sad and unfortunate accidents. This is the part of life that cries out for vengeance – for some kind retribution. The anger, the desire for revenge seem to demand it!

Yes, the hurt, the pain and the injustice is so understandable! But what is the alternative? Would you want to put the perpetrator(s) in your shoes and force them to feel the pain – the anguish – the deep sorrow? Then what? Would that change the way they are – the way they feel – the way they think? Nothing can EVER be forced! But do remember – there is a final accounting for EVERYONE! There is a final justice!

TRY to forgive "whatever" it is – whomever it is – and get on with living life! It is not easy to forgive a deep hurt – an unbearable sorrow, but it **is** possible. Find the JOY and don't let go! Do it, not only for yourself, but for those you love – for the health of our earthly planet – for the sustenance of our entire universe. Know that every action and thought is written in the Akashic records for all eternity! As the great seer, Edgar Cayce, once stated, "not one jot or tittle" escapes. (I take that to mean not even one period or comma in the story of our life is overlooked.)

Enlarge your soul capacity to "see" further:

Appreciate the nobility and strength of your body.

Celebrate the brilliant capacity of your mind.

Bless that giant reservoir of emotion and memory you possess.

Refuse to allow hatred to eat away at your very soul!

Destroy the anger before it can destroy the inner beauty you possess!

Then watch how you begin to GROW in wisdom, inner strength and eternal understanding!

THE LANGUAGE OF THE STARS

You are now in the Age of Aquarius! Astrological knowledge is here for everyone to understand. This metaphysical science is meant for anyone who wishes to understand the mysterious journey they are on and the meaning of life on this earth plane.

Astrology is a science involving the Signs of the Zodiac, the Houses of the natal chart and the Planets with its aspects. All this will show how their cycles and their electromagnetic vibrations affect you. Awake or asleep, you are subconsciously feeling the planetary vibrations stimulating you – interacting within every moment of life. Sometimes, much to your dismay, you may act foolishly, or with anger or sudden impulse. Your higher self knows us better, but still, you feel helpless – you feel out of control! Yet, at other times, you give so generously of your kind and good nature. Why?

First, you need to understand the language of the stars – the planetary vibrations that fill our universe. Observe what they can teach you. Please keep in mind, your astrological chart was not haphazardly designed. Your time, date, birthplace, and parents were all part of a definite plan – your plan to guide you in living your current life and to assist you in facing your challenges as well as fulfilling your dreams.

You are a partner in this birth-death cycle. The whole point of it is for YOU to gain the opportunity to develop a greater awareness – to gain a deeper understanding of yourself and the world around you – to share your many talents and to help your human family all around the globe. In many cases, it may be to take care of "unfinished" business on this earth plane. In others, it may be a fulfilling life, long overdue. To be born was, in part, **your** decision, not just arbitrarily assigned to you.

Astrological knowledge points the way to understanding the **how, why and when** of your life. Furthermore, understanding your astrological background allows you to breathe the rarified air of **true awakening** – to find the freedom of spirit, of body and of mind. **Understanding** your astrological chart can greatly assist in **understanding** the **mysteries** of the **how**, **when** and **why** of your very life plan!

WHAT ARE PLANETARY CYCLES?

As you look back on the various situations of your life, you may very well discern a certain pattern of coincidences that seem to repeat themselves within the framework of your lifestyle. Have you not sometimes thought, "Oh, this has happened before" or "Here we go again!" Have you not wondered if such a situation could be further avoided or even lessened in difficulty and stress? Why do we keep making the same mistakes? You are not alone! The entire human race goes through this. Fortunately, there is help available through many, varied sources. One great source, that proves to be very valuable, is the astrological one!

Armed with the knowledge of your natal chart, you will be in the position of understanding the planetary cycles. Astrology is an ancient science, developed eons ago, as far back as Atlantis and Lemuria. It is the planetary song that vibrates within each one of you. Your astrological chart is a living, breathing design you created. It encompasses the total plan of what you have brought with you. Your parents were the instruments that allowed you to come forth on this planet and passed on to you what you needed for your genetic disposition, and early childhood development.

The study of the planetary cycles connect you, electromagnetically, to every sensitive point in your natal chart. These sensitivities highlight your strengths and weaknesses, creating a pattern that can be traced with accuracy. This is a metaphysical science that goes well beyond the boundaries of the five senses. It describes your mental, physical, emotional and soul capacities – your life plan! The planetary cycles will plainly guide you in understanding what you have come to achieve and what you have come to overcome! There is, indeed, a destiny plan for each of you on this swirling ball of oceans, mountains and plains.

Would you not want to understand your planetary arrangement?

Would you not want to understand your weaknesses, abilities, strengths, and tendencies to which you are prone?

Astrologically, the SUN is the most powerful influence of all. It is the pivot of your astrological chart.

In the physical world, you cannot live without the light of the SUN or survive without the streams of its life-giving energy.

In your own inner world, your Sun-Sign represents the real you – the inner self – the spirit and essence of YOU.

The rest of the planets have cycles as they revolve around the Sun. Everything on this planet, from the great bodies of water to the minerals, the animals and we human beings are affected by all these great bodies of energy.

Consider the magnetism of the moon, alone (controlling all the tides of the earth). With patience and diligence, you will discover that the timing of situations in your life will correlate to the movements of the Sun, the moon and the planets as they transit your natal chart.

Identifying these happenings is what astrology is all about! Carl Jung, the great psychoanalyst, called it synchronicity. "As above – so below".

The magical key is once you understand your planetary patterns, individual to you from birth, you will be far more capable of understanding the situations in your life that will come along. Why? Because your attitude will grow in understanding and patient timing. You will be in better control of your own life. In a nutshell, you will begin to rise above the mundane and you **will** begin to see the big picture. Part of that picture is seeing and understanding your own inadequacies and impatience, much of which may need pruning and change.

Now you are in charge – now you have a handle on your life. You no longer need to get stuck in old patterns and old thinking! Every life has its high and low moments. The fact that they can be plotted and studied for greater illumination is miraculous! Imagine how wonderful it is to be able to SEE where you are going, and to be able to ANTICIPATE reactions within yourself, thereby being able to handle them more efficiently and honestly.

Identifying and understanding the current planetary cycles against the backdrop of your natal chart is the intelligent way to approach astrology. There is no mystery or magical power here – only the studied and mastered art of synthesis. Your natal chart is your own "special timing mechanism" impregnated into the "intelligence" of your every cell at birth. When you begin to understand the vibrations to which you respond, you will have come a long way in prudently handling those unpleasant and repeating circumstances you are so familiar with. Then **YOUR FREE WILL** can be used with wisdom and discernment!

Learn your Planetary Cycles – and watch how your life unfolds!!

RIGHT TIMING

We live in a world governed by **time.** Time is the basis for everything! We eat, sleep, plan and dream by the clock. We live by that eternal "buzzer" in the morning and by the late news shows at night. Time is the measure, the guide and the taskmaster of everyone! Have you ever considered how astrology is deeply involved in the science of timing? The cyclic pattern of the planets at the time of your birth, coupled with their current cyclic movements of the current day, is the heart of your natal chart. As you parade through the various circumstances in your life, you begin to realize how important **timing** is to achieving success and happiness.

I am sure you all can identify people who are so fortunate as to be in tune with themselves a great deal of the time. As you observe them, you will find their natural sense of timing (whether it is patience, gentle caution or an innate understanding of the situation), helps them through many difficulties that the rest of us would simply muddle through with a "woe is me" attitude. Why is it that some people seem to know when to make the right moves and when it is the right time?

Perhaps their harmonious timing within themselves could be better understood if you could see their planetary configurations at birth. These massive planetary vibrations form "energy patterns" and, most likely, some of these patterns were quite harmonious (from an astrologer's point of view), at birth. Strange as it may seem to the logical mind, you DO respond to the planetary vibrations of your natal chart. Your reactions DO correlate with those energy patterns crystallized at birth. Remember, I said CORRELATE not CONTROL!

Indeed, the subject of astrology does bear examination to see what value there is in unraveling the mystery of your nature. The more smoothly the energy patterns flow in your natal chart, the easier it seems to be to "time" your actions in a useful and constructive way. The energy drive inside you must be harmonious before anything on the outer level (physical world) can be harmonious. That, is what the planetary cycles, at birth, will indicate.

"Right timing" is so important! How we so **want** to live a life free from tension and needless worry. Yet, many of us bounce along, on each insecure wave of emotion, and are left exhausted upon the wreckage of storm-tossed relationships – too rushed and anxious in this daily life of living.

This means you are constantly reacting to the inharmonious vibrations within yourself. Once you recognize these cross-vibrations, you will be able to review the repetitive situations of your life that continually frustrate you. Right timing will stop being an elusive dream and become a real possibility!

Once you become familiar with your energy patterns and the unique way you respond to them, the sooner you will be able to learn to master responsibility for your actions and reactions.

Then, your timing will be harmonious from your own developed self-discipline and a greater understanding of your life plan!

★ Freedom comes when you begin to understand yourself, accept yourself and love yourself (with all your idiosyncrasies).

★ Freedom comes when you realize what planetary cycles are working within the confines of your inner, psychological nature – and realizing what seems to trigger your inharmonious responses.

★ **Freedom** comes when you are in tune with the marching rhythms of your life.

Then, you can time your actions and reactions with prudence and common sense.

Then, you will utilize your natural ability to discern the "right time" for action and the "right time" for cautious refraining.

WHAT IS A NATAL CHART

The place, as well as the time you were born is extremely important. It crowns your entry into this life. Astrologers calculate the longitude and latitude of the place and time you were born to "recreate" a picture of the heavens at that time. This is not an arbitrary grouping. It is a precise photograph of the planetary positions at the time of your birth. This is what the astrologer studies in order to arrive at some clear perception of your natal key, your natural instincts and your inherited tendencies.

To recapture the exact planetary patterning of your natal chart, the accurate birth time (within four minutes) is necessary. With the vast recorded birth information today, many people have access to this data and consequently to a wealth of information waiting them. If you do not have access to this birth information, do not fear. A solar chart is also very revealing. (Please see Solar Chart next).

These planetary patterns are radiating electromagnetic vibrations that impress themselves within your very core being. I am talking about energy. You will become sensitized to these vibrations for a lifetime. They will stimulate you, for lesser or better, depending upon your outlook, your understanding, and your tolerance for self. Everything you say, do or think requires energy. You have mental energy, physical energy, emotional energy and spiritual energy. This energy life force is everywhere around you as well as constantly moving within you. To use Albert Einstein's words, they are "pulse-like concentrations of fields, which would stick together stably". This is the stuff of life!

How many times have you used energies in ways you later regretted or felt you had no control over? The truth is you can always be in command of your energies, if you but apply the will. Your use of free will is the "way" you use your energies, either constructively or destructively. It is a poor excuse to say, "My stars are not right today" or "I was born with a terrible chart!" No chart is ever terrible! You cannot be forced to do anything except when you allow your own free will, through ignorance, indifference or lack of understanding, to be manipulated.

By interpreting the positions of the planets at birth and by understanding their interacting vibrations, you will have a marvelous tool to better comprehend the intricate pattern of energies that lie within you. It will help clear your vision and open your understanding. This is why birthdays are so important! It is not so much the passage of time remembered as it is the time you entered this world. It is momentous, indeed, as each of you are so special and unique. Day or night, north or south, east or west – your birth chart represents a key that can unlock many of your frustrating mysteries. Your birth chart, once understood, will lead you to a greater freedom of understanding that precious "inner you".

THE SOLAR CHART

No Recorded Birth Time –What Then?

Since a natal chart needs the time, date and place of birth for accuracy, many people become discouraged when the true time of birth cannot be found. For these people, let me comfort you by saying that a solar chart can be used when the correct birth information is not available. It can be drawn with your Sun-sign as the focal point. That is, you start with the Sun-Sign on the first house. The placement of your planetary arrangement will then be viewed and analyzed from your Sun alone.

Remember, your Sun and the sign it was in at birth will radiate throughout all you think, say or do. The Solar chart is significant proof of this. Why? As the physical Sun is the center of our universe, our source of light and life energy, then so is your own astrological Sun, positioned at your birth, the "center" of your own universe, the central force of the 'real' you! Therefore, it is possible for an astute astrologer to interpret your life plan through the eyes of the astrological sign your Sun was positioned in when you were born. The astrologer can also see the Sun's relationship to the rest of the planets and a valid interpretation can follow. It is not as detailed as the natal chart, but it is still a very valid chart!

Remember, we are studying the energy patterns you have radiated to from the time you were born. Since the movement of the planets is a slow process, from day to day, with the exception of the Moon, and perhaps, Mercury and Venus, we can understand much valuable information from just the position of the planets in your solar chart alone. You may also ask, "What about those thousands of people born on my birthday? How can we all be the same?" First, you do share common planetary patterns and common energy vibrations.

However, please remember there is always the modification of time (where in the world), place (what longitude and latitude), background (types of parents), attitude (education, and early childhood experiences), and individual reactions to life experiences according to your soul memories.

Personally, I have found solar charts to be vital and filled with information when people cannot find their birth time. Even twins, born at the same time still have "individuality", despite the common energy patterns and common backgrounds. Even twins have different reactions. They are still individuals with free will like anyone else. Although solar charts can never replace natal charts, they are quite revealing and helpful in their own way. Astrological knowledge never ceases to amaze anyone who studies it when they discover how many ways this knowledge can be utilized and applied to "practical living".

THE LUMINARIES, THE SUN AND THE MOON

We Need the LIGHT in our Lives!

Astrologically, and spiritually, LIGHT is a powerful factor in our lives. Therefore we need to be very aware of its influence. The Sun and Moon are unique for their primary energy is light and the reflection of that light.

The SUN

Astrologically, the Sun is the most powerful influence of all. Just as the Sun, physically, is the center of our universe, astrologically, it is the central force of your natal chart. You cannot live without its light and its streams of the life-giving force. The entire universe revolves around the Sun. Symbolically, the Sun represents your true "inner self", the real **you**, the spirit and essence of you! Therefore, through the sign of your Sun at birth, its energies will radiate through you constantly. This is your Sun-Sign.

The Sun represents the vital, active WILL centered in the heart!

The MOON

Astrologically, the Moon is but a reflection of the Sun's rays, mirrored back to you in the darkness of the night. As the Earth turns away from the life giving energies of the Sun, the Moon will shine, luminously and with gentler rays, illuminating the darkness with tenderness. Therefore, the moon becomes, in astrological terms, the sensitive, reflecting vibrations of your moods, emotions and soul memories. We so need to understand these rays of gentle light.

The Moon represents the emotional tentacles of FEELING,
you reflect back to the world!

WHAT IS THE MYSTERY OF THE ECLIPSES

Eclipses have always intrigued the human imagination simply because they are an unusual phenomenon produced naturally. Here is a situation where the absence of Light sends a message.

The Denial of Light

The Solar Eclipse

The solar eclipses are the most dramatic, as they occur in broad daylight and are produced only by nature. The drama begins with a noticeable change in light and pressure. As the light becomes obscured – with the passing of the moon over the Sun, the temperature drops. You are being denied the warmth and life-giving properties of the Sun, even if only for a short time.

This solar phenomenon occurs at various times. It is a marvelous and yet unnerving sight. A total eclipse is where the body of the moon slowly moves in front of the Sun and eventually blocks out all of the Sun's rays with an enveloping black shadow. It will suddenly seem as night, in the very middle of the day. Nature itself becomes confused. Its internal clock is suddenly off balance. Even birds stop singing and there is an ominous feeling. There are partial solar **eclipses** also, where the darkness on the sun is limited, and its significance depends upon where the shadow falls on earth.

The area of this shadow, whether total or partial, is what astrologers consider to be of the greatest importance. Through observation and analysis, astrologers have learned that such an event has repercussions. The solar eclipse, may remain mysterious in meaning for many months. Finally, when a transiting planet crosses that point of the eclipse at the time the shadow occurred, then that part of the world where the shadow fell upon would be affected. That trigger point of the transiting planet, moving over that exact moment of the solar eclipse ignites a promised event. This would be a crucial time for that part of the world. The solar eclipse has been understood to indicate some form of ending for the ruler or leader of the country where the shadow has fallen.

In the ancient days, total solar eclipses were not understood. When the total Sun was blacked out at high noon, terror was felt throughout the land where the shadow covered. The ancient peoples were mystified by such a happening and eclipses were always interpreted as the "wrath of the gods" coming upon them.

Perhaps one of the most significant, historical solar eclipses took place during the heated battle between the Medes and the Lydians. It took place in Asia Minor in the early summer of 584 B.C. As mid-day approached, without warning, day turned into night. The opposing sides threw down their weapons and fled for their lives. Suddenly nature was larger than the realities of war. Perhaps this is why the military of ancient times always consulted an astrologer to guide them when in battle.

The Lunar Eclipse

There are also lunar eclipses, both total and partial. This is where the moon is blocked out. The lunar eclipses seem to indicate the condition of the people of the country where the shadow falls. Remember, the shadow is interpreted as the lack of light. Something is being denied. Upheaval, change and problem-solving need to be brought out into the light – into the consciousness of the populace – for change is due as a lunar eclipse affects the people of the area where the shadow falls.

In the case of a lunar eclipse, a most significant one affecting the people of the United States, was the assassination of President John F. Kennedy. A well known astrologer, at that time, pinpointed a most sensitive degree in the United States chart that was affected by the lunar eclipse at that time. This degree of the eclipse indicated extreme danger to the White House and of course, the people. Remember, lunar eclipses affect the people of the country where the shadow falls. Americans lost a beloved leader.

The earliest record we have of eclipses was in 2205 B.C., initiated by the Chinese ruler Ta Yu. Even back then, the observation and study of the heavens was taken very seriously. We all know that any dynamic action of the Sun or the moon can cause certain physical effects such as tidal waves, earthquakes, typhoons and volcanic eruptions. Perhaps, if we studied this phenomenon more closely, the eclipses could reveal much more about the inner warning systems of nature.

CHAPTER TWO

THE TWELVE SIGNS OF THE ZODIAC

The TWELVE SIGNS of the ZODIAC

Aries ♈

Taurus ♉

Gemini ♊

Cancer ♋

Leo ♌

Virgo ♍

Libra ♎

Scorpio ♏

Sagittarius ♐

Capricorn ♑

Aquarius ♒

Pisces ♓

THE ZODIAC

The Zodiac is divided into twelve parts called the Signs of the Zodiac. It is an invisible arc in the heavens said to extend eight degrees on either side of the Sun's path.

In this area lies the constellation of stars with which we are familiar. These signs originally came from the constellations in which these stars were grouped. The word, Zodiac (Greek in origin), means circle of animals. You will see that the majority of the sun-signs have animal symbols. Remember the importance of symbols!

THE SUN-SIGNS

The astrological year begins with the sign of Aries. Starting with March 21st, the Aries' characteristics will dominate for that period of 30 days. All Aries' traits take precedence, influencing those who have the Sun and any other planet(s) in that sign. And so it goes, for each month and sign of the Zodiac the Sun is in.

In astrology, the intensity of the Sun's rays are measured and interpreted in various ways. Since the Sun is the physical center of our universe, then so, symbolically, the Sun-Sign you were born under will reflect the qualities of the real "you" – the heart of your individual world – the center of your inner self. The basic characteristics attributed to each Sun-Sign will describe common denominators for all born under that sign. Today, many people do not know what their Sun-Sign was at birth. So let's find out when a Sun-Sign becomes a Sun-Sign. The following chart will help.

Aries	March 21 - April 20
Taurus	April 20 - May 21
Gemini	May 21 - June 22
Cancer	June 22 - July 23
Leo	July 23 - August 23
Virgo	August 23 - September 24
Libra	September 24 - October 22
Scorpio	October 22 - November 22
Sagittarius	November 22 - December 22
Capricorn	December 22- to January 20
Aquarius	January 20 – to February 19
Pisces	February 19 – March 21

Understand well – This is not information I expect you to accept blindly!

I encourage you to read and investigate further. Observe yourself, your family, your friends and anyone else around you. Listen to them! Watch their actions and reactions! Examine their approach and behavior as described in each Sun-Sign. Let the detective in you go to work! You will be amazed at the synchronicity of each individual's Sun-Sign qualities and the tendencies of their behavior. Astrological knowledge speaks for itself. We do not have to defend it or champion it. Its practical knowledge will amaze you.

The Special Importance of Your Sun-Sign

As you proceed, you must always keep in mind that the sign the Sun is in at the time of your birth – your Sun-sign – is most important to you!

As the physical Sun is the center of our universe – your Sun and the sign it is positioned in – is the center of your own universe! It is your most important signpost. It will describe the manner in which you utilize your basic life force! Indeed, your Sun-sign will indicate your soul lesson and echo certain qualities and characteristics that are vital to you!

Important: The purpose of this section, is to assist you, the reader, in grasping the essence of each sign. We will be discussing the essential character – the inner core of each Zodiacal sign. The twelve descriptive signs will ALL have meaning in your life pattern because they are all in your birth chart to some degree. However, the strongest meaning will come from your Sun-Sign. Once you have grasped this understanding, you will begin the mastery of astrology. Therefore, let's start with the first baby steps – the first piece of your magnificent puzzle – the meanings of the twelve Zodiacal signs and, in particular, your Sun-Sign!

ARIES

March 21- April 20

The First of Three Fire Signs

An examination of the traits of the Aries sign, common to all born with the Sun in Aries (March 21- April 20), will show certain similarities. Let us now observe, analyze and attempt to perceive the heart of the Aries nature.

The Aries type people always seem to be in a perpetual whirlwind of energy and motion. Being a FIRE sign, they possess the quality of fire. They can energize and warm the "cold shadows" of timidity and injustice in an instant!

The Aries type people have the attributes of part strength and part aggression – part force and part dynamism – always pioneering and always positive! If this sounds like leadership, then you are correct. Their innate tendency to take charge is enormous. Fighting for what they believe in (sometimes at the cost of reason) is a significant badge of the Aries courage.

By understanding the Aries characteristics, you will be comprehending one-twelfth of the basic traits of the human race. This sign description reminds us of the crusader in modern dress – the vigorous pioneer in thought and action – the individual with enough initiative to lead an army. Indeed, these are some of the magnificent traits of the Aries vibration.

Of course, the Aries type people are not all saints. There is a lesser vibration they can radiate to, just as there are two sides to every coin. They can be foolhardy and attempt things well beyond their scope, circumstance or ability. Moreover, people with a strong Aries vibration must be careful not to approach anything with such a one-sidedness that other people's opinions and feelings are neglected or overlooked.

I do not believe this is intentional on their part. Indeed, they must learn to forbear! Even the thought of failure seems impossible to them. They must be careful their enthusiasm does not carry them (or anyone else they are in contact with) away on the fast moving tide of ardent fervor. They hardly seem to be aware of the possibility of being swamped with the overwhelming waves of zealous action – or the uncontrollable tide of potential negative reaction. They only seem to look straight ahead, with blinders on, so their focus is not distracted.

If this is not your Sun-sign, and yet, somehow you feel a kinship with some of these qualities, then somewhere in your birth chart, wherever the sign of Aries lies, there are these corresponding influences that do affect you in your own life pattern. This will depend upon the Aries placement in your natal chart, the planets involved and its aspects. That will be the area where you will feel these similarities mentioned above.

THE RAM

(Seek the essence of this sign)

The Ram has always been the traditional pictograph for the sign of Aries.

It is indeed fitting, for the Ram is the "leader" of the flock. Symbolically, the Ram describes the dominant features of the Aries vibration. They are the features of one who thrives on leading, directing, pioneering and initiating.

Just as the beginning of spring coincides with the beginning of the astrological year (March 21), you will find a connection between this astrological sign of Aries and the physical rays of the Sun. The life energy of the Sun's rays in the spring, are so potent it encourages seedlings to sprout, even though the ground is still hard from the winter crust. Is this not symbolic of the vibrant determination of the Aries type people – leading others through difficult moments of life with courage and determination? Perhaps, now you can understand a little of the power of the Aries vibration and the power of the Aries SUN.

Just as the Ram (with its huge, curled antlers of authority) gives direction to its group, so does the Aries type person take charge and can inspire others with their energy and enthusiasm. Again, if you feel an overwhelming tendency to lead or instinctively gravitate toward a pioneering attitude, then most likely there is a powerful influence of Aries in your natal chart, be it the Sun, moon or any other planet.

The symbol, given to each sign, holds much to meditate upon. As you begin to comprehend the true characteristics of each of the Zodiacal vibrations, your understanding will deepen, as will your perception of human nature. You will be touching part of the key to the very riddle of life! It is with this clear awareness of your strengths and weaknesses that you will be able to develop the tolerance and patience so needed in dealing with yourself and others, compassionately. Then, watch as a greater harmony builds within you – a greater tenderheartedness.This is so needed for the higher evolvement of our world.

Hopefully, when you give thought to the natural tendencies of the Aries type people, you will be able to accept them as they are and where they are. From their point of view, they do not see that they can be combative or aggressive. These ways are as natural to them as breathing. Being highly competitive, they will want to be the best and get there first! It's doing what comes naturally to them, whether it be sports, business or pleasure.

Of course, a great lesson will imprint itself on the Aries type person at some point in his or her life. They will realize that in order to lead, they must have a flock – those willing to be led. An innate sense of purpose pushes most of them forward with ram-like energy, but often there is little careful thought or planning. If they can learn to couple forethought with drive, then such a combination will produce invaluable service to humanity. Such a marriage will shine with enduring worth. This is the capacity of the Aries nature!!

If you have an Aries type person amidst you, take a good, objective look at their ways and tendencies. Try to understand them in the light of its pictograph, the Ram. If they seem quite dominant, understand they must express themselves if they are to be true to themselves. At the same time, they must also learn to consider the opinions of other people. It is only because they become so engrossed in their own aims and desires that they fail to heed others around them. Only objectivity will balance their intensity! It is this objectivity that will help to produce outstanding leaders – leaders whose valor and inspiration will make them treasured individuals.

The Keywords for Aries

I AM

Did you know that astrologers learn a great deal about people when they listen to the words they use in ordinary conversation. Invariably, the Aries type people will use their key words "I AM" constantly. The "I AM" is indicative of the fire quality of Aries. It has a deep spiritual connection to the Divine Source. This astrological sign rules the head, that part of the body that houses the pituitary and pineal glands – the seat of our intuition, and our spiritual connection to the Godhead. "I Am that I AM." There is a great mystical truth here. Aries is the first sign of the Zodiac, and carries the creative seed of divinity we all possess!

Think about these keywords for a moment. Say them out loud a few times with some force. There is a certain power and a confidence that seems to exude with each forceful repetition. Many Aries type people start a conversation with "I am positive", or "I am right" or "I am sure". The 'I AM" is a constant reminder of the positive individuality they feel within themselves when relating to the rest of the world. Sometimes, their cocksure and aggressive manner, exemplified by the words, "I AM", indicates how confident they are that their way is the best way. They always seem to be filled with the creative energy and the enthusiasm to accomplish what they want.

Unfortunately, there are times when the attitude of these keywords may be viewed as opinionated or one-sided. But for the "I AM" people, that is simply the way it is! They know they are important! They are telling the world, through their keywords, here and now, that they are alive, vibrant and confident and all will be well. Since their words indicate forceful thought – then only forceful action can result. This is why the "I AM" people are the doers of the Zodiac. No one can ever stop the true Aries type individual from expressing him or herself. They will push their way to the front (as the Ram does) and take charge! They will perform and achieve rather than dream or think.

However, do not be misled by such a voicing of individuality. The most powerful lesson for the Aries type people is co-operation. It is as essential as their need for leadership. Impatience can also lead to problems. They must be careful not to overdo, or push too hard in setting and attaining their goals. Cooperation is the balancing keyword for them. They must learn teamwork! They must consider other people – other opinions – other ideas. If not, they will find no one to lead!

If you were born sometime during the Aries time span and feel no kinship with these qualities, then somewhere in your natal chart there must be a "blockage of energy", preventing the flowering of such abilities. The Aries type people move where others fear to tread. They create and achieve with astonishing speed and energy. They possess all those wondrous qualities of optimism and self-assurance. The "no problem" attitude is **always** a constant.

So, go find yourself some Aries type people. Listen to their words. Out of their very mouths, they will identify themselves – clearly and honestly.

★They are the I AM people of the Zodiac.

★They are the pioneers for their more faint-hearted brothers and sisters.

★They can accomplish what many only venture to dream.

★They possess the fire to dare to do what others only hope for

★They will continually inspire you to never give up !

ARIES is one of the three FIRE signs –
ARIES, LEO & SAGITTARIUS

TAURUS

April 20 – May 21

The First of Three Earth Signs

In the lovely days from April 20th to May 21st, the entire part of our hemisphere regales in the lushness of young green with the earth sprouting life in leaf and stem. Yes, Taurus is an earth sign. The month of Taurus is filled with the brilliance of color, birdcall and perfuming blossom. Mother Earth is approaching her peak, bestowing her natural generosity with breathtaking beauty. Forsythia hedges sparkle with yellow and fragrant blooms of fruit trees echo the haunting perfume of nature. Thus, we begin to glimpse the artistic and lush beauty of the Taurus vibration. How rooted they are to the precious Earth!

Remember, there is a strong correlation between the sign of the Zodiac and the path of the great Sun as it parades through that Zodiacal sign of each month.

The Taurus type people love beauty! Indeed, the Taurus vibrations function extremely well on the physical, earth level. They love to grow things and possess a strong sense of nurturing. I call them the "Green Thumb" people. It seems whatever they nourish in the plant world responds magically, indicative of their natural kinship with Mother Nature. Perhaps it is all part of their being an earth sign.

They have a keen eye for beauty, especially in the physical dimension, be it sound, color, taste, smell or touch. They could be called the connoisseurs of the five senses. They have an instinctive love for beauty in all dimensions whether it be the curve of the human body – the sound of an exquisite violin – or the palpitating beauty of a breathtaking sunset.

Since the Taurus type people have precedence over the throat area, many of them have lovely speaking voices and a deep sensitivity to music. This is a Venus ruled vibration. All that is lovely enters in here. The physical appearance of the Taurus type people is earthy and obvious. Their eyes and hair are luxuriant and their sense of dress is usually tasteful and practical. They are very fond of all the "good things" in life, denoting pleasure, enjoyment and comfort.

In the business world, the Taurean vibration has a perfect head for utilizing the most systematic approach for success. This quality is found in many bankers and financial institutions. They possess an excellent business sense and make dependable and wise workers in this area. Security is, also, invaluable to them. The power and value of money, with its many uses, is wisely appreciated. Many times, they will tuck away a nest egg for a "rainy day" unbeknown to anyone. This is a MUST in order to keep a sense of security. It also reinforces the need to be comfortable and independent, should such a time arrive.

Another remarkable quality of the Taurus type people is their intense loyalty and devotion. They are faithful friends and their dependability, in times of stress, is an absolute haven to others in need. These practical people have a no-nonsense approach. When times get difficult, they keep what they have and would never think of scattering their energies uselessly for situations not grounded in the practical world. This earth sign is rooted (note the word) in fact and common sense. Consider them like the "Rock of Gibraltar" – enduring, real and very strong.

As the Arians are the natural pioneers of the Zodiac, so the Taureans are the natural settlers of the Zodiac. Stability and realism are their watchwords. Go find yourself a Taurus person and observe his or her ways. Notice their reactions to situations that arise. Reflect on their practical approach that accompanies these reactions. They generally have a kindly, placid nature and move with comfortable pace and ease. Admire the marvelous gift they possess in creating restful and harmonious surroundings.

On the other side of the coin, you must understand the principal Taurus tendency which they must learn to overcome. It is change! Once their minds are made up, they find it difficult to change. They can become obstinate. Their stubborn nature moves with steady, rock-like endurance and they will absolutely resist if anything disturbs their comfort and equilibrium.

THE BULL

(Seek the essence of this sign)

The Bull is the traditional symbol for Taurus. Since there is a strong significance between the symbol of the sign of the Zodiac and that sign's characteristics, let's consider the qualities of the bull. The Bull is known for its strength, tenacity and endurance. It is a fearsome animal to contemplate because of its fierce but seldom shown temper. On the other hand, it is a most docile, gentle creature when left to its own business. It enjoys the simple life. This description can also apply to the Taurean nature.

Taurus type people have a gentleness, and easy-going manner. They live in the everyday world. Practical inclinations are overriding, geared to the earthy, physical pace of their daily journey. However, under that seemingly quiet nature lies a powerful force of determination. Nothing, but nothing will deter them from pursuing their goal once their mind has been made up. With patience, and piece by piece advancing, they will not back down, even in the face of awesome obstacles.

Indeed, they will hang on with bull-dogged persistence and unrelenting purpose.

Many of you, who deal with Taurus type individuals will find them to be, at their greatest intensity, plain stubborn. This truly seems contradictory, since the qualities of the Taurean nature, are so versed in common sense. Yet, they can go to the limit in obstinate resistance if they are pushed. This is the other side of the easy going Taurus nature. Here is their greatest lesson – to learn it is necessary, at times, to give way to others and not get stuck in a mold of unreasonable tenacity. This tenacity is magnificent in time of real need, but most difficult in situations where cooperation is necessary. They need to understand that releasing a hold is not a sign of weakness from within, but a **prerequisite** for cooperative effort. Strength of purpose needs to be balanced with reasoned consideration!

Indeed, we have much to learn from the Taurus type people. They have remarkable characteristics that give a clear guideline for practical living and honest realism. To them, facts are facts, and day dreaming is a non-entity. For the others of you, not so realistic, or practical, or grounded in the essentials of daily living – perhaps you will begin to appreciate the golden thread of "common sense" by observing and emulating the admirable Taurean qualities.

The Keywords for Taurus

I HAVE

The "I have" is well sprinkled throughout conversations with the Taurean type people. I HAVE is certainly indicative of their thinking and approach – a steady reminder that they view themselves as secure and happy when owning something, or accomplishing something in the physical world. "I HAVE this" or "I HAVE enough" are real because they live in a material world, understanding its practical demands. There is a genuine need for Taurus type people to hold and possess property, acquisitions and bank accounts. This is not for show or aggrandizement. There is a real need for security and it can only be expressed through the medium of the physical world. These are the vital signs for the "I HAVE" people – the down-to-earth people.

We call them the "business men and women" of the Zodiac. The value of money and all it entails – the value of ownership and all it entails – is guided by their practical nature. Unfortunately, when others view this as too materialistic, they need to understand that Taurus type people generally do not love money for its own sake. It is only a necessary means to provide them with the earthly comforts and possessions they so dearly love.

Practical they are! If there is a deal to be made or business to be garnered, the Taurus instincts will sense them and move in with sure-footed skill. It is their down-to-earth philosophy that helps to maintain a steady and calm outlook. The "I

HAVE" people can always be counted on in a financial pinch. They continually seem to have the reserve to draw upon.

The great lesson for the Taurean nature is to learn that the goods of the earth are to be used, not possessed! Everything, even affection, can never be bought or owned. Possessiveness, in the light of balanced living, must constantly be examined. Hopefully, you can now understand how the I HAVE people **need** that feeling of ownership. Without material comforts and security, they can experience a hounding sense of failure and lack of well–being.

Watch the Taurus type people and listen to them. They are trying to tell you something important about themselves. Having and holding is very vital to their well-being. If you find you radiate to the Taurean qualities and were not born in the month of Taurus, then perhaps you have a planet in this sign. Wherever Taurus is in your natal chart will be where you radiate these qualities. At any rate, there is a great deal to learn from the I HAVE people, who daily plant common sense and nurture security with everyone they meet.

★They are the I HAVE people of the Zodiac.

★They are the sensible, down to earth, realistic individuals.

★Their love of beauty is deep and constant.
★They are the practical, hard headed thinkers.

★Their friendship is true and lasting.

Taurus is one of the three EARTH signs –
TAURUS, VIRGO & CAPRICORN

GEMINI

♊

May 21 – June 22

The First of Three AIR SIGNS

In examining the characteristics of the Gemini nature, keen observation becomes a critical necessity. This is about the qualities you may exhibit if you were born with your Sun in the sign of Gemini, or if you have a planet/s in the placement of Gemini at birth.

Being an air sign has a special quality all its own. At times, it is quite easy to take for granted, or underestimate the marvelous versatility of the Gemini nature. Perhaps, the best recognized trait of the Gemini is the ability to speak fluently, if not copiously, on just about **any** subject. Their desire for information is voracious. Their versatility is constant. They can be charming, quick-witted and fun to be with.

The Gemini vibration always seems to be moving into newer fields of thought and experience. They cannot tolerate dullness or boredom. They possess an insatiable desire to know things – many things. "Jack of all trades, but master of none," is frequently used to describe this vibration. However, that is not completely true. Many Geminians are brilliant scholars and strong producers in the arts and sciences. Their minds are quick, elusive and highly cerebral.

The Geminian Sun-sign indicates a strong receptivity to training and education. However, the racing of their minds, quickly filling with ideas and plans, can cause them to lose much in the way of concentration. Most writers, speakers, teachers, advertising people or anyone else given to the power of the word would have a strong Geminian influence in their natal chart. Their world is the world of communication – especially in the commerce of everyday life.

One important area they need to be aware of is the way they use their nervous energy. This incessant nervous energy seems to spill over with either enthusiasm or boredom. Many times, this energy is in danger of being wasted in needless tasks or projects that have taken their fancy for the moment. Being so versatile both in hand and mind, they just love to have two things going on at once! A whirlwind of activity constantly surrounds them.

Being an air sign, you must realize that the quality of air cannot be contained or captured – it is free and wide roaming. So it is with these Gemini type people. Whether it is a place, idea or situation, it will not matter. This restless, indecisive and very charming vibration needs to be always moving, talking, thinking and responding. The freedom of being unencumbered and mobile is everything to them. This gives them the adaptability they are known for.

Perhaps the greatest pitfall for these Gemini type people is the difficulty to settle down and stay with one thing at a time – or at least until it is accomplished satisfactorily. Restless children of the Zodiac they are! However, at some point (hopefully when they are younger), their greatest learning lesson will be not to start a second project until the first project is finished! If not, they will lose the battle to utilize their fine abilities if they tend to follow any whimsical inclination that seems to come their way. Since the thinking power is their greatest attribute, stability of thought is what needs to be cultivated.

At any rate, go and find yourself some Gemini type people. Observe them – their words – their actions. At times, these words or actions can resemble floating bubbles sailing through the AIR from the pipe of versatility and endless imagination. But, as bubbles dissipate, all too quickly, it would be better for them to develop the instrument that creates the bubbles rather than to be immersed in the bubbles themselves. They need to cultivate perseverance. Inner calm and deliberate discipline are essential to their well being!

THE TWINS

(Seek the Essence of this Sign)

The pictograph for each sign of the Zodiac has deep symbolic meaning. The Gemini characteristics are vividly described by The Twins. There are many ways to depict the Twins. They also can be symbolized in other pairs, such as two pathways – or two columns. Whatever the symbolism – there are choices to be made!

If it is the twins, the first twin represents mortality, explaining the vulnerability of man, and the second twin represents the spiritual self, the higher consciousness seeking to steady the instability of the other twin. This signifies the duality of the Gemini nature!

Another symbol used frequently are two columns (one white and one dark) symbolizing the polarity of positive and negative. There are two sides to everything. The Gemini individual needs to make this comparison consciously. It is only through comparison that the Gemini vibration can make decisions. Although this comparative nature makes them appear vacillating, indecisive and insecure. The truth is they are grappling to understand their own style and method.

★We need to be patient with these mecurial individuals, who move with lightening speed.
★We need to be patient with their high rates of energy and abundant mental fertility.
★ By comparing, they learn –
by comparing, they understand –
by comparing, they grow!
Give them time and space and patience. This is how they learn.

Usually, this nature of duality has a steady influence in their lives, such as two professions, two situations, two opportunities at once, two ideas pouring out. Many things come in pairs for them, always forcing them to make a choice! I have read some damning statements about the Gemini characteristics, including their indecisive and flighty nature. Please, try to understand the Gemini type person and the way they function. There are two sides to everything. They, themselves know that. They also know that indecision is the other side of comparison. However insignificant or tantalizing a decision is to you, to them it is all important! They are constantly pressed to make decisions all their lives. Often, they wonder if they took the right course (again, we find indecision). Remember, it is harder on them than it is on you!

How they do sparkle with their ideas and verbal abilities. Monotony is deadly to them! They may even become depressed if there is no adequate variety of experiences, ideas or travel to challenge them. We are dealing with the conscious mind here. Self-discipline is necessary! They cannot give in to superficial skimming just for variety or color.

They need to exercise their intelligent perception, so readily available to them. Once they have developed their abilities to communicate and express – be the artist's palate – the writer's notebook – the mechanic's tool or the salesman's persuasive style (to name a few) – their Gemini nature will truly shine with multifaceted ability and the astonishing brilliance of mind power.

The Keywords for Gemini

I THINK

I THINK are the key words that exemplify the mental abilities of Gemini people. If you listen to their conversations, you will invariably hear the "I Think" words flow constantly. Indeed, the I Think people are highly visible with their animated chatter and profuse ideas. They love to laugh and joke – their vibration being light and quick. Mind power is everything to them. Within their mental frame, persuasive ideas can flow like the heavy rain during sudden downpours..

"I think this" or "I think that" or "I always thought" – and so they spin their web of ideas and dreams. If, at times, they seem to chatter endlessly – realize they are trying out their mental wings. As fledgling birds learn the pitfalls of wind currents and preying beasts, so the Geminian type people must guard against the draining of their precious mental energy from fanciful illusion. The I THINK people really do try to see both sides to everything! Although they may vacillate from one side to the other, thoughts flying at breakneck speed, they truly have a hunger to understand and know everything! Again, they must be careful of the Jack of all trades, master of none syndrome. Like finely tuned instruments, their delicate nervous systems can go out of balance easily. Yet, they can be **so** adaptable – so easily trained in many areas of life – so flexible, agile and above all, interesting!

Therefore, go search out some I THINK people.

★Listen to them and appreciate their versatility and their huge capacity for life.

★Encourage them to develop one thing at a time and to patiently see it through.

★Appreciate the splendor of their minds as their need for comparison trains it.

★The world so needs the vivacity and enthusiasm of the Gemini individual.

They are at their finest when communication is directed with purpose!

Gemini is one of the three AIR signs –
GEMINI, LIBRA & AQUARIUS

CANCER

June 22 – July 23

This is the First of Three WATER SIGNS

For any of you born within this time span of June 22 through July 23rd, your Sun will be influenced with the vibration of the sign of Cancer. If you feel kinship with the characteristics described below, but were not born in this time span, then chances are you have a strong planetary placement in the sign of Cancer. In describing the Cancerian traits, you surely must realize, by now, the distinctive difference between each sign of the Zodiac.

The Cancer type vibration is very emotional, in every sense of the word. Feelings are everything to them – whether they understand this consciously or not. Many times they "feel" a situation or condition through osmosis. This means that understanding seeps into their awareness in a very subtle way. They will somehow have a 'feeling' about whatever is going on. Remember, this is a water sign and water means emotions and feelings.

As the moon, ruler of the sign of Cancer, seems to look over the earth in a protective fashion, so do the Cancer type people want to protect and guide others. Both a Cancer type male or female will want to "build a nest" wherever they settle – wanting the permanency of home, or home-like conditions to keep them contented and feeling secure. Their settling instinct is most constructive. With patience and diligence, they will build, manage, and provide for the future with a usually consistent and practical nature. They are extremely conscientious, domesticated and thoughtful. Their memories are phenomenal.

However, at times, a worrisome nature does seem to hound them. Of course, being home builders, they will want to plan for the future in order to build a sense of security. This is all important to their well-being – as essential as breathing. Yet, these gentle souls will immediately start to worry about the outcome of any situation before it even begins!

Having a kind and unprovoking nature, these Cancer type individuals do not like to fight or be combative. The tendency here is to take the path of least resistance – to not make waves. Sometimes this tendency can give way to moodiness or despondency. Usually, they feel helpless or unhappy if they are bound by difficult circumstances. However, they will fight like "unchained tigers" when their homes or family are threatened.

Fear is the great enemy of Cancer type people. Predisposed to clannishness, they fear the unknown, especially for their family. These tender souls always want the best for their offspring. They do not like to venture into uncharted territory, but content themselves with the comfort of their home and the sanctuary of their personal lives.

Being a water sign (meaning emotional in astrological terms), they are quite susceptible to the moods and conditions of people around them. When they feel moody, for no reason, they are most likely tuning into someone else's fears. Cancer type people come into this world with strong psychic abilities. As a result, they can experience all kinds of feelings due to their extreme sensitivity. Not only can they reflect the positive feelings of others, but can also mirror the instability and unhappiness of others. Cancer type people are shaped by their impressions, their surroundings and their relationships. It is important for them to understand this in order to erase that sense of worry that can hound them.

Being the gentle souls that they are, they must learn to develop inner strength when fear crowds in and panics their senses. Help them to shake loose and let go their own suffocating dust of past memories – their own endless debris of hurt feelings! Exaggeration, imaginative anxieties and numbing hesitation can also be common adversaries.

The Cancerians, however, do possess an amazing strength of tenacity. Apart from their delicate feelings, they can be quite a tower of stability in a wild and rushing society; creating a haven for those who need a home and yearn for quiet safety. Indeed, the Cancer traits are the bulwark of our country's foundation. The United States has a birthday in July – the Fourth of July! Can you now understand the home-loving tendencies of this nation and its protective desire for family life?

THE CRAB

(Seek the Essence of this Sign)

Perhaps you are wondering why the Crab is the universal astrological symbol for such a home-loving and protective sign as Cancer. Let's examine the characteristics of the Crab and see how it reveals the inner workings of the Cancer type people.

The Crab, being a creature of the sea, wears a soft shell that offers little protection for its innate timidity. When Crabs are frightened, they run to the nearest rock for safety (their home-like fortress). So Cancerians also need their home atmosphere as a buffer against the daily battering of interaction and confrontation with others. The peace and solitude of their home is as necessary to them as breathing is for human life.

Fear is the enemy they must learn to deal with – fear of the unknown – fear of the future – fear from the past, still lingering with them. Fear can become a monster that can distort their imagination, sometimes rendering them helpless and ill. Being so sensitive, they are very vulnerable to "suffer the slings and arrows of outrageous fortune" as Hamlet so pondered in a typical Cancerian mood in Hamlet by William Shakespeare.

A difficult lesson for the Cancer type people is learning to part with personal claims – to surrender personal feelings. They can cling to these. They can smother with over-protectiveness. They must let go and realize there is a loving influence at work in the world.

Deep emotional responses help make them a most valuable member of the Zodiacal family. They are very responsive to the needs of others. They care about you! They are considerate, sentimental and gently loving. What a wonderful comfort in times of need. They seem to know, instinctively, how to erase burdens and share your sorrow – whether it is on a family or personal basis – or on the world-wide scale of human tragedy.

Just as the Crab is open to every preying creature in his ocean home, so can Cancer type people be "slaves" to their unrestricted emotion. It is this sensitivity, this receptivity that exposes them to the constant turmoil and excitement of daily living. They FEEL vibrations all around them. Sometimes, these vibrations are so subtle that others less sensitive are completely unaware of their existence. So, like the Crab, they must learn to withdraw from disturbance.

They must learn to create an inner world of peace where no one else can enter. It is this inner peace that will keep their equilibrium and help calm the "unstable" waters of flowing emotion. Walk gently around the Cancer type individual. Return to them a little of the consideration that marks them as comforting companions in a world of harsh reality. Do not overlook them because their considerate and thoughtful ways are so soft and gentle. DO NOT take them for granted! They are the stabilizers of all family life!

Above all – please remember, as the crabmeat is the sweetest in all the ocean kingdom, so are the Cancerian traits the ones dearly remembered!

The Keywords for Cancer

I FEEL

Cancer type people are really a joy to listen to in conversation. They are so easy to recognize. Their keywords, I FEEL are used with predictable consistency. Their feelings are always out there with "I feel that" or "I feel good" or "my feelings on that subject". Their world is measured, examined and interpreted by FEELINGS.

The Cancer type people are so extraordinarily sensitive that they can be psychologically vulnerable to criticism and ridicule. As a result, they have highly developed and protective instincts in order to feel their way along in situations. Whether they are charming or considerate – moody or melancholic – their feeling tentacles are out there all the time. Even decisions are approached in this manner. When they think about something, it is their "gut feeling""that surfaces to guide the final decision. It is their "gut feeling" that seeps through as a result of the absorption of the environment that surrounds them. It is their "gut feeling" that is the true measure of action and reaction for them.

Their fertile imagination produces great story tellers. However, this fertile imagination can also cause them to be prone to worry. Even before something happens, they will be concerned about the outcome. They are thinking and feeling way ahead of what can go wrong. It is imperative they develop positive attitudes. Anything negative – be they thoughts, fears, or emotions – can churn their insides like a windmill caught in a windstorm.

The I FEEL people are a kindly lot. They are very taken with the family clan – the family tree – the family nostalgia – the Family PERIOD! It is an all-consuming interest for them. They love to reminisce, cherishing the sweet moments of yesteryear – the faded photographs of childhood. These I FEEL people are really gentle souls who walk with pyschic antennae – feeling their way as their emotional responses guide them. It is this very quality of sensing that develops their excellent ability to deal with the public. Instinctively, they seem to know what people want – what they need – and how to please them. Indeed, they are "people" persons.

Cancerian children are a delight, even though their impressionable nature can be heavy for them when they are young. Patience is required (in large doses) because their timid nature can easily be dominated. Sometimes their wonderful imagination can run away from reality. But their pleasant dispositions do mark them as delightful children.

Actually, the I FEEL people are the most comforting of companions. They are usually very constructive in their efforts, unless beset by moods or unknown fears. In dealing with the I FEEL people, you must allow them the dignity and respect their sensitive (moon ruled) emotional nature longs for.

★Honor the gentle, nurturing quality of the Cancer type people.

★Appreciate their consideration and caring.

★Cherish their sustaining qualities for home, family and country.

★Where would the human race be without these comforting and nesting qualities?

When they say "I Feel", believe me they do, right down to their toes!!

Cancer is one of the three Water Signs –
CANCER, SCORPIO & PISCES

LEO

♌

July 23 - August 23

This is the second of three FIRE signs

As the stately Sun continues its processional march through the pacing months of the year, you will find its fiery path approaching the sign of Leo. If you feel comfortable with the qualities of this Sun-sign, then chances are you will have the Sun, the moon or any another planet(s) in the sign of Leo at the time of birth.

Those who are influenced by this Leo vibration exhibit the dynamic and most dramatic qualities of the Zodiac. Leo type people pour forth their affection and display their emotions openly. They will frequently shower you with emotional hugs and hearty back slaps. How the greatness of their vibration seems to flow! Everything is done in a "big" way. No mean, small petty things for them. Their affection is as large as their appetite for fun and pleasure. They can love unselfishly and with passionate abundance. Lucky are those who bask in the warmth and demonstrative love of the Leo. Remember, they are a fire sign and need to glow!

The Leo type people are fun people! Possessing an exuberant nature, they want to take care of your every need to insure your happiness. Such positive light flows from them that others naturally tend to follow. They seem to command spontaneous devotion from a world that loves charisma and charm.

Organizational abilities are inborn. Leo type people have the ability to **take charge** and systematize any situation or circumstance. Coupled with their magnanimous nature, they are easy choices for positions of authority. Their wide, sunny smiles are obvious trademarks. They smile with such a joy that seems to radiate their vitality. How they do shine! Since the Sun is in the Leo sign, there is an affinity – a deep need to shine, like the Sun. Never – never **dim the light** of the Leo type person. This is the kiss of death! How they need to shine and warm – to protect and enlighten – to amuse and entertain! If they are not given the opportunity to exhibit their true selves, they will soon find misery a constant companion.

There is another side to this astrological sign that is rarely duplicated in any other sign of the Zodiac. It deals with the heroic tendencies that surge through the Leo nature. These tendencies, which enhance their aura, are probably due to the strong sense of obligation they feel to those under their care. (Lawrence of Arabia comes to mind with his vibrant Leo Sun) Magnanimity issues forth from the very core of their heart center. They excel at cheering and encouraging others. They are great with children. There is an easy rapport with them, knowing instinctively their needs. Indeed, the enthusiasm and gallantry of the Leo type people lifts the spirit and encourages the more faint-hearted. Their ability to organize and lead is very indicative of this fire sign.

Once secure, natural self-confidence flows from within them. Confidence will promote the security of knowing they can do anything – that they do possess heart as well as skill. Strong conviction will pervade their consciousness. Their **will** becomes absolute and unmoving. Instinctively, they will sense the right time to act, preferring to lead as the head of the group rather than as a subordinate. What they do need and seek are opportunities **to shine**! Again, never – never dim their light!

Pride seems to be their Archilles heel! They cannot stand to be humiliated! Striking any blow to their dignity crushes not only their vitality, but demeans their efforts (which really comes from the heart). Please remember, they will work their heart out for you – but you must appreciate and treasure their efforts. How their passionate, dynamic leadership is so needed today, within the hectic pace of modern living. Once the Leo type people learns to overcome the ugly monster of pride, then as true leaders, they will never again be swayed by egotism.

THE LION

(Seek the Essence of this Sign)

The magnificent pictograph for the sign of Leo is the **Lion**. By examining the nature of the lion, you will be able to understand the tendencies of these individuals who are born under such a vibration. The Lion can be the most ferocious animal, and is often considered the king of the jungle. He is the strongest and sometimes the most feared of all the animal kingdom. Other animals respect him and give him wide berth. Please take note of the majestic bearing of this animal and his grandiose gait. He walks with the restraint of a true king, with flowing mane, so wondrous to behold.

Leo type people have this same, innate ability to walk tall and with dignity. They seem to command the very space they enter. Indeed, a certain majesty seems to wrap around them like an "invisible cloak" of royal design. However, if their loved ones are attacked (or their personal loyalty questioned), they can be fearsome! Yet, their generous nature can make them easy prey to the more cunning members of society. Because of their earnest belief in others, Leo type people cannot seem to fathom anyone stooping to low and mean ways. Actually, the higher type Leo still finds it a shock when other individuals around them act with pettiness and cruelty.

Living and working with Leo type people is always an adventure. They shower forth an abundance of warmth and affection in a never-ending stream of attention. However, they require (almost demand) this same attention and treatment from others. Their ability to love is overwhelming, at times, molded by a fiery passion. They must be careful to give this love with discrimination. The heart must not lead the head – which, unfortunately, can often be the case.

The dignity of the Leo type people never fails to impress. Exuberance and shining confidence do make them the hypnotic "pied pipers" of the Zodiac. Their dramatic sense of timing gives them the edge in holding attention and maintaining loyalties. Actually, they themselves are quite loyal and give forth a protective quality of comfort and safe–keeping to those under their wing.

Even though, at times, they do seem to overestimate (or over dramatize), this lavishness can be quite consoling when others move about in fear and anxiety. Somehow, the potential of power of this sun-sign continually seems to impart strength and gallantry. Admirable warriors – decent and kindly in spirit – they carry forth a part of the human race in grand and magnificent timing. They coordinate and organize with ease and understanding. Indeed, their generosity precedes them with an outpouring of affection to "warm" a cynical world!

The Keywords for Leo

I WILL

These keywords, I WILL, send out powerful and dominating signals. This attitude and approach is admirable and quite successful. Whenever you listen to the Leo type people, their determination and strength of will flashes forth. "I will go..." or "I will make it easy..." or "You will do it". The I WILL people exert a strong influence upon those around them. They possess such a driving force (fire sign) for success that they can actually WILL it. Since their uncanny ability to organize from chaos allows nothing to go unchallenged, they will proceed through life searching and exploring the great arena of will.

No one can pressure them to conform. Their powerful I WILL nature refuses to be subjugated or repressed. If their will is questioned, they gather their energies and fight. They will use their WILL to energize any task and to inspire all comrades.Always, their WILL remains supreme.

However, if there is denial of joy or lack of opportunity, their natural confidence can suffer a blow! If their needs are not met – they cannot shine. If they are hidden in some obscure corner of life or relegated to some menial task – they become very, VERY unhappy. To feel self-realized, they function best in positions of authority and responsibility.

The I WILL people have a real love for life.

Being highly creative, they will seek access to pleasure continually. They feel it is their essential birthright to love, laugh and gamble for higher stakes. The gambling instinct is also part of their daring nature. The most humiliating disgrace for the Leo vibration is losing face! This is a mortal blow as their pride and dignity are easily bruised. However, perhaps the greatest lesson for the Leo type individuals is to learn to share their talents without demanding. They do demand obedience as well as loyalty.

To cross their will is deadly. Sometimes, they lack the understanding that other people must be considered – that cooperation is the essential to the "fabric of life". You can help the I WILL people to realize that true devotion comes only from a willing heart. That their own loving and generous nature WILL produce the loyalty and devotion they seek, naturally, and in its own course of time.

You can also help them to realize the need to regroup their energies – energies they give off so spontaneously – so generously. Here is the opportunity for you to transmit the love and affection to these Leo type people – the love and affection they so need themselves. Help them to assume the nobility of leadership they carry so well – be it in the "heart of the home" or the "desk of the executive".

So, go find some I WILL people. They are abundantly surrounding you. Watch them and listen to their words. Quickly, you will find how they **do** identify themselves.

★They are the magnificent actors, ebullient lovers and benevolent parents!

★These qualities are all precious parts of the Leo signature.

★These are the life roles they fulfill with a dramatic flair unequa led to any other sign of the Zodiac.

Their expansive, loving nature – open, grandiose and generous to a fault – lighting the way to the simple joys of life.

How they can SHINE like the sun!

Leo is the second of three FIRE signs –
ARIES, LEO and SAGITTARIUS

VIRGO

August 23- September 23

This is the second of the three Earth signs

The time for the Virgo influence comes as the Sun glides through the pleasant days from August 23rd to September 23rd. Virgo type traits are emphasized. Again, we are not only talking about the Sun-sign but other planets that may be positioned in the sign of Virgo at birth.

The Virgo type people have tendencies that are most pronounced for others to see. Their natural vibrations are usually gentle. They are often recognized by the "quiet expression" in their eyes and their "precise manner" of movement. Their keen analytical disposition supersedes in most anything they do. Deeply conscientious, thoughtful and reserved, they seek to be useful in every way. Their practicality places them among the most valued of workers, being very dependable when "clutch hitting" is needed.

The Virgo type people need no spotlight. They do not want it. They delight in working behind the scene. They want to clean to the very corners of every task with tidy effort. They desire efficiency at every turn. The Virgo traits also include a fine ability to assist others with a conscientious attention and a strong sense of duty. Research is another area where their painstaking attention to detail is appreciated. I want to call them the Mr. and Ms. Clean of the Zodiac.

Perfection is their goal – their high aim – and their deepest frustration. As we all must realize, at one time or another, perfection is just a fragile dream! We do live on an imperfect planet. We are here to work toward perfection! But, to the Virgo type people, perfection is sought, both subconsciously as well as with open awareness. If it is subconscious, then they always seems to have an irritating feeling – an inner quality of unhappiness – a sense of poor accomplishment. If it comes with an open awareness, then the frustration is obvious and disconcerting.

Because of their sensitive and fastidious nature, there is a tendency to worry and fret when excellence eludes them. The desire for perfection compulsively takes precedence, be it a job, a one-on-one relationship, or any other effort they are involved in. They will always be wishing it could have been done better, or more efficiently or with greater honesty. I call this a "scrub-board" conscience since this approach can cause most Virgo type people to become insecure, destroying any seed of self-confidence they may have built.

Although there is a strong inclination to see imperfection in others, their own imperfection hangs heavily in the vision of themselves – obscuring the good they actually do accomplish. It seems they cannot help but look back at situations and fret as to whether they did all they really could when in reality, they probably did wonderful things.

The Virgo type people are “finely tuned”. They are delicately balanced between the practical approach to life and the constant seeking of the perfect. They are the true devotees of wisdom – forever searching, sampling, examining, analyzing and discriminating. Remember, they always seem to be searching for the elusive shape of perfection in others, when they really seek it for themselves!

Because of the delicacy of their nervous system, their health can suffer, even though they possess a keen interest in good health and strive, through a sensible diet, to live a rational life. Instinctively, they seem to know the importance of maintaining good health. However, some of them must be careful that health matters are not blown out of proportion. They can easily become hypochondriacs. Many times they are found in occupations related to the health ideal.

As you contemplate the Virgo vibrations, you will find prime examples of principled and devoted individuals who desire to be of service to others, be it on the intimate scale of personal relationship or on a global scale of human service and devotion to all.

THE VIRGIN

(Seek the Essence of This Sign)

Each pictograph continually gives off a subtle portrayal of the inner meaning for each sign of the Zodiac. For the Virgo it is the attractive symbol of a Virgin carrying golden sheaves of wheat. The Virgin maid signifies the virtuous and gentle nature of the Virgo type people who seek "purity" in every sense of the word – from food, to relationships, to ideals. The golden sheaves of wheat indicate the attainment of wisdom in the earthly, practical sense – seeds for the staff of life. This meaning is closely related to an existence with the built-in desire to serve in the highest sense.

This practical earth sign is often happier when working under the direction of another. Although the Virgo type people may appear cool, reserved and quite matter-of-fact, they are really gentle and giving in their own distinctive way. They are not demonstrative, possessive or demanding. They have a simple and direct manner, and are usually reliable, dependable and very, very steady. Of course, they are fastidious, whether cleaning a room or searching for answers. Compulsion is to be avoided! The sharp tongue and the observant eye can make for an uncomfortable companionship if the Virgo nature is vexed about disorder or lack of cleanliness. Harping or nagging or any other continued verbal tirade can turn the most gentle of the Virgo type into a demon of reprimand and impatient reminders.

Hard work and a deep abiding sense of purity (perfection) seems to hound them. Their sense of excellence can create profound intellectual waves, from the cultural to the scientific. Their fine mental capacity for detail and thoroughness continually goes through the sifting of analytical scrutiny – strained again in that inevitable pursuit for perfection.

Being an earth sign, they have a tidy way of moving and thinking that keeps practical living on an even keel. However, sometimes their microscopic analysis of life makes them extremely critical. Remember, they are guided by system and order.

"A place for everything and everything in its place" is a philosophy they subscribe to, willingly.

Help these wonderful souls to be patient with others. Help them to understand that they must be even more patient with themselves! They must be careful that a brilliant performance is not clouded with the narrowness of outlook. Perfection is the ultimate they seek, but in the process, they must take advantage of their logical thinking, and their incredible common sense. Do not miss the forest for the exact description of the trees!

The Keywords for Virgo

I ANALYZE

The keywords for the Virgo type people is constantly heard in their conversations. "As I analyze this" or "Let me analyze the situation". We must realize these people function in the mental world of comparison, deduction and analytical dissection.

It is this discerning mental faculty that causes them to be conservative in their actions, as well as their ideals. Most Virgo type people marry later in life because of this very analytical standard of perfection. Often their tenderness and simple approach is disguised by their harping censure and critical eye. They seem, at times, to have no tolerance for those who do not try to help themselves. They so respect the work ideal and admire the work ethic.

These keywords, I ANALYZE, are most indicative of the head leading the heart – worrying and fretting that all will go smoothly in perfected rhythm. Fanfare, notoriety, bright lights are not the "measure of success" for them. It is the knowledge that their job is well done, smoothly and with best effort. That is their reward!

The I ANALYZE approach seems to precede them in every aspect of life. They scour the mind with cleaning pads of conscientious energy. They pumice motives with detailed effort. They scrub and comb attitudes and methods with the determination of a sanitation code. The I ANALYZE qualities will always continue to shine with efficiency and dependability. How they love to be diligent and faithful in any endeavor – be it a spotless home or an ecologically perfect earth.

Indeed, these key words are the concise embodiment of the Virgo type qualities. As with the Gemini type people, who never seem to stop their own mental faculties from working overtime, their Virgo type partners move with steady persistence into the direction of perfected effort. Both these astrological signs share the planet Mercury as their guiding planet. Mercury simulates the vibration of communication of all types.

You can assist the Virgo type people to better understand themselves by encouraging them to not be so critical of their own efforts. Help them realize what great examples they are to the rest of the world. These I ANALYZE people are quiet, dependable and always there. They may never send out rockets bursting with excitement or take charge to lead, but they do bring, to the human race, a magnificent lesson in perseverance, duty and faithfulness.

★The Virgo type people are the shining examples of service to others in every sense of the word.

★We all can learn much from their ways that hum with the harmony of precision.

★Virgo is the earth element of caution, practicality and realism.

Therefore, go find some Virgo type people and listen to them.

Once you understand them, you will begin to deeply appreciate them and be grateful for their presence.

Virgo is the second of the three Earth signs –
TAURUS, VIRGO & CAPRICORN

LIBRA

♎

September 23 – October 24

This is Second of Three Air Signs.

Time moves on as you progress through the year's calendar. As the rays of autumn sunshine filter through the sign of Libra, we find it is a time of elegant weather – crisp, clear and rich with the full blush of nature's golden stage. As you begin to understand some of the harmonious vibrations of the Libra nature, you will also begin to see the correlation to the beauty of the autumn season.

The Libra type people are "people persons", too. That is, they enjoy companionship, social gatherings and all social contact. It is a distinctive vibration – one that constantly seeks balance and harmony. They tend to want to be in the center of things – keeping vision open for both sides of any issue or situation, seeking always to find the balance for correct decisions. If they seem to vacillate, or fluctuate in opinion or feeling, it is all in the name of fair judgment. They are feeling and judging their way to fairness. This is what they seek! They must be sure!

There are times when such decision–making can exasperate a partner or friend (who must wonder why situations never seem clear-cut to the Libra vibration). But, to the Libra type people, it underlies their deep concern for justice. Before any decision is made, a clear conscience must be resolved within themselves. They must be fair, honest and true for they are the natural peacemakers! They exhibit a very strong will in this regard.

You will most likely find Libra type people in the position of litigating or bargaining, weighing and balancing, back and forth. They are forever seeking the middle ground of compromise. They realize, more that any other sign of the Zodiac, the need for impartial and realistic thinking, in the name of good and fair judgment. These individuals are excellent at arbitration. This is what they always seek! They must be sure! They start off with vacillating or fluctuating opinions. Others must understand that situations or problems are never clear-cut to these Libra type people.

Perhaps, if you understand their deep concern for justice, then you will understand that before any decision is made, they must resolve within themselves that it is fair and true. This particular quality of the Libra type people is perpetually sustained throughout their lives. Being natural peacemakers, they are forever seeking compromise and harmony. They understand, more than any other Zodiacal sign, the need for balancing – that there are always two sides to everything. These people are excellent at arbitration.

They, also, are a refined breed. They are usually called the "beautiful people" as they seem to be born with engaging features and naturally refined ways. They possess an enduring love for beauty, for lovely surroundings and for fashionable dress that seems to set them apart in a rather elegant mold!

Being true devotees of the cultural world, be it theater, classical music, ballet, art or any other intellectual or artistic pursuit, they possess good taste, a delightful and considerate manner and usually a cultured, knowledgeable background. Anything unclean or disagreeable could cause them to turn cold and uncooperative. These reactions to unpleasant situations or conditions may seem odd to such individuals who always seek balance, but these reactions will surface immediately under any inharmonious conditions or surroundings.

Despite their seemingly calm exterior and cultured interests, they do possess a will of iron. A perfect analogy for the Libra type people is the iron fist in the velvet glove. Once they are resolved in their decisions (although it may seem forever for them to decide), they will press on with dogged determination – committed to their principles and sense of fairness!

Observe the Libra type people around you. I am sure you will soon discover their charming and aesthetically inclined nature. If circumstances allow, you may even find them becoming deeply involved with some cultural achievement. Observe them closely. Watch their decision making approaches – and know they are trying to make the end result always fair and equitable, in accordance to their abilities!

THE SCALES

(Seek the Essence of This Sign)

The pictograph for the Libra vibration is the scales of justice. This symbol is most impressive. Is not the total of life's experiences always weighed and balanced in the final outcome? Do you not feel a real desire to live more harmoniously and with a cooperative nature despite the pull and tear of the difficult realities of living?

I believe the Libra type people, especially, radiate strongly to a peaceful co-existence! It is an absolute necessity for their well-being. They do not like discord! The surroundings must be harmonious for them to function well. If they have to deal with discord persistently, it can actually affect them physically, causing them to become ill. That is how sensitive their nature is to a lack of harmony. As with the pictograph of the balancing scales, everything in life needs balance. Even as the health of the physical body works through the kidneys, these kidneys resemble the scales and actually are the balancers of the body. Their job is to filter and eliminate impurities to keep the body in balance. In astrology, Libra does rule the kidneys.

The companionship of other people is also vital to their well-being. They understand, all too well, that we cannot live alone in this world. As a result, they may marry early, since they love companionship so dearly. They possess the eternal wisdom to know they need others. It is an all-consuming, indispensable requirement.

The Scales represent two parts of anything that must be balanced. Only by being fair and cooperative, can situations, arrangements or decisions be kept on an even keel. In everyday affairs, the Libra type people will try to see both sides with equal impartiality. They will search to seek a wise and proper solution – be it on behalf of a child's quarrel or a judgment in a courtroom. The ancient Egyptians used the Scales as a symbol of the weighing in of the sum total of life's deeds at the time of death. Indeed, balancing is such a delicate art but such a vital necessity to life!

I am sure you are aware that everything has two sides, two points-of-view. We all learn to discriminate on this earth plane through the method of comparison. The Gemini type people exult in comparative thinking, but the Libra type people utilize this comparison to produce a fair decision, which they want to end in harmony and balance. They are both air signs, dealing in the world of thought. The Gemini vibration deals with the conscious mind, and the Libra vibration (now encompassing the personal consciousness of the previous six signs – Aries through Virgo) deals with the subconscious mind on a broader level.

★The first six signs of the Zodiac (Aries to Virgo) function within a personal level – the inner world.

★The last six signs of the Zodiac (Libra to Pisces) function with other people – the outer world.

For the Libra type people, this equalizing act does well with individuals on a one-to-one basis. Their natural grace and refinement lends itself easily to the art of diplomacy. They excel in counseling, legal work, and anything that beautifies the earth and its inhabitants. They strive continually to make living an elegant retreat – searching for compromise and cooperation in a world that seems steeped in egotism and willfulness.

The Libra vibration has an instinctive need and a great depth for understanding the need for balance. Remember the scales! Watch them – they can teach us all!

The Keywords for LIBRA

I BALANCE

Of course, the Libra type people do not go around saying I BALANCE. However, frequently, in conversations, you will hear "Let's cooperate", or "That's fair", or "I can see both sides".

Relationships are very important to the I BALANCE people. Is not cooperation part of the delicate art of balancing? When you seek to compromise, when you try to settle situations so each part is satisfied, then that must be the consummate act of good judgment. Behind every such scenario, you will probably find a strong Libra type person generating it. Perhaps, this all comes about because the I BALANCE people know they need others. They do not like to do things alone! Companionship is as essential to them as oxygen. In their desire for acceptance and approval, they are more inclined to seek a balanced solution to a problem, than go it alone.

Whenever a powerful, dominating planet moves through the sign of Libra, relationships will be affected. This will be the time when the true meaning of relationships, partnerships and cooperative exercises go through a drying out on the clothesline of grievances and empty affiliations. Many Libra type people will find their own lives deeply affected. What does it mean? It means that with true cooperation and balance, the final result will be a greater freedom and understanding for everyone involved. It means that the artificial clouds of misty relationships could be blown away. It means that NEW attitudes may have to be developed for meaningful relationships. A rebirthing process could be in order! Cooperation is the keynote! There is a lot to learn from the I BALANCE people.

The sweet, quiet exterior of the Libra type people can often mislead you. You will soon realize that once they have made up their minds, they will move with sure-fire speed to accomplish what they feel is right. They may begin their wail with "I do not know what to do", but always seem to end with, "This is the best solution". In between those two statements, they are in a mental juggling act, comparing both sides to see what would be the best and fairest course of action – whether it is the purchase of a crystal goblet or negotiating an international treaty. After spending some time in deliberation, the "balancing act" is completed and the decision is made as fairly as possible.

The gracious nature of the I BALANCE people is always a delight. Regardless of how strong you may come on, they will try to exert diplomacy and skillfully maneuver the most difficult situation to their liking. Allow the Libra type people and their intelligent discretion to help you. Their thinking and their approach can assist you in reaching harmonious conclusions.

In the coming years of change, the Libra desire for compromise and proportioned agreement is what we all need. We all can learn a great deal from the Libra type people. Their amicable, urban ways – their pleasant, charming smiles – their winning, refined manner are all part of the special Libran type traits – a durable, elegant polish this tarnished world sorely needs!

★These Libra vibrations lift the heart and enhance the grace of the soul.

★These Libra vibrations connect the essence of relationship to its highest.

Libra is the second if the three Air signs –
GEMINI, LIBRA & AQUARIUS

SCORPIO

October 24 – November 22

This is the Second of Three Water Signs

With the days shortening and the shadows lengthening, you will now find the astrological Sun has shifted into the sign of Scorpio. The Scorpionic tendencies and characteristics may well describe a part of you, even if your Sun placement is not in the Sun sign of Scorpio at your time of birth. Why? It may well be you could have a strong placement of other planet(s) in the sign of Scorpio that does not include the Sun at the time you were born. Remember, there are also eight other planets, as well as the moon, traveling in the path of the Zodiac at that time.

It would not be overstating to say that the Scorpio type people are often quite misunderstood. I have read some very damaging statements about this sign – a sign that, in reality, holds much promise and great power!

As nature signals the clue as to the subtle interpretation of a sign, you will find this to be the time of year when the life force in nature begins to "retreat". The gracious leaves have left the trees bare. The approaching winter is becoming a reality. The sap starts to seek its own resting place before the heavy cold begins, winding its way into the hidden, dark comfort of nature's roots.

Characteristically, we find the Scorpio type people similarly retreating in the many instances of their life. There is a certain reluctance to expose themselves! Their feelings and thoughts are kept deep within and they exhibit a clever ability to save for the crisis periods that may lie ahead. Their cool, silent and hidden qualities are the dominant ones. Not given to small talk or to frittering away time or energy, the Scorpio type individual will hold, gather and wait until the time of real need for action comes! Then, with the strength of Samson, they will move forward to their goal with bold decision and determination.

Actually, their silent ways are very important to their sense of protection. It is needed to build their self-confidence, in privacy. Once you understand their disposition towards hiding (and even burying) their feelings, you will begin to understand why they try so hard to protect their emotional vulnerability from others. SILENCE is their defense!

Their reticence is not from lack of interest or boredom. They are sparing of words, reserved and self-contained, because to reveal their emotions is to be naked and defenseless! That is how sensitive and vulnerable they feel. Is it then understandable as to why they are not too open and candid about their true feelings?

They hide the depth of their emotional intensity under the "quiet watchfulness" of a bodyguard; policing an unfriendly crowd. Yet, their courage, once ignited, is dauntless and their endurance steadfast. It is their psychic sensitivity that is surefooted and keenly perceptive. What a wonderful detective streak they possess – probing with a cold and deliberate approach when necessary. "Still waters run deep" aptly portrays the intensity of their hidden emotional fire. A determined, feverish drive will crown their efforts, but tormented jealousies and resentments will demean them.

Nothing is lukewarm about the Scorpio type people. They love to ponder upon the mysteries of hidden things, having a natural propensity to ferret out secrets. Their emotional capacities are volcanic. They will either be devoted friends, or enemies to be feared. Extremism, in both points of view, is everyday bill of fare for them.

Their physical appeal is very magnetic, being very attractive to the opposite sex. Their penetrating gaze – their subtle magnetism can create a hypnotic charm that seems to bind the object of their attention. This physical attraction never seems to wane. Their charisma is undeniable. There is no question that the Scorpio type people hold much power and inner strength to "influence" those around them for good or otherwise.

THE SCORPION

(Seek the Essence of This Sign)

Please note: this sign also considers the Serpent, the Eagle and the Phoenix Bird.

The scorpion is a form of insect known as an arachnid. It is widely feared for its poisonous sting. However, it is quite unfair to use this symbol as the only pictograph for the sign of Scorpio. I believe this sign was the principal symbol originally, since the Scorpio type people were poorly understood. There are several other symbols that possess just as strong a kinship with the characteristics of this sign. They are the serpent, the eagle and the Phoenix Bird.

First, let us took at the scorpion and examine why this insect is associated with the sign of Scorpio and even given its name. Upon observation, you will notice that certain tendencies of the Scorpionic nature do seem to carry the deadly sting of sarcasm and revenge. If the Scorpio type people are disturbed in their drive for whatever they seek, they will reach out and retaliate (generally in an emotional and vindictive way) against those who thwart them. The fearsome sting of the scorpion symbolizes the intensity of emotion and the volcanic power of desire that sweeps through the Scorpio vibration.

The second symbol for Scorpio, not often used, but quite valid in its meaning is the serpent. Throughout the ages, the symbol of the serpent has been used to universally represent wisdom. In some philosophies, the serpent power portrays the "kundalini", the energy force that rises up the spine to eventually reach the crown charkra. This is the spiritual force that facilitates the enlightenment of human beings. Perhaps this will give you an idea of the depth and concentration of the Scorpio type people and their need to solve mysteries (the greatest being the life and death states).

As you begin to appreciate the Scorpio potential, you will understand a little more about their remarkable abilities to delve into the mystical and to raise their creativity to the spiritual level.

The third symbol is the eagle. The eagle soars to the highest in flight. A proud and dynamic energy possessing great distant vision and its physical power of strong wings.

The fourth and greatest symbol for the sign of Scorpio is the Phoenix Bird! This is the symbol of a bird that rises from burnt ashes to be reborn again! This is the distinguished signature of transformation and rebirth! Scorpio people have a healing power that can bring regeneration and hope to others as well as themselves. It is part of their nature.

The Scorpio type people are indeed complex and mysterious. Individuals born with these strong vibrations can allow their intensity to injure others with their harshness of tongue and vindictiveness of revenge, or they can exhibit an enormous capacity to heal with their love alone! They do have the ability to energize their powerful vibrations into amazing constructive channels. It is their deep, emotional capacity of love – their magnetism that can send healing, not only to themselves, but to others anywhere in the world. We all have this ability! (Check your Scorpio placement in your chart).

As each sign shows a propensity for positive and negative drives, we must leave it to the Scorpio individuals to utilize their most concentrated power, stimulating to the very core of the regenerative life force. You can assist them by encouraging the "milk of human kindness" to flow more easily within themselves. You can help them to realize they NEED to TRUST more – to shape their feelings with gentler understanding. Such a need and such a shaping can transmute any earthly desires into a great spiritual force.

Leaders they are, but in a most indirect way. Brilliant examples of devotion at its heights and fierce tenacity at its prime, these individuals can tap the creative energy of the universe at any time. They can demonstrate, to the rest of the world, the endless flow of healing that can gush forth from every human being. Remember the sign of Scorpio is in everyone's chart. In what astrological house does your healing ability lie?

The Keywords for Scorpio

I WANT

The keywords for the sign of Scorpio has traditionally been "I want" or "I desire". These keywords give you evidence of the intense desire nature they possess. The I WANT people want so badly, that at times they are unable to control their desire nature. Thus, they soon find themselves in a whirlpool of confused emotion, dragged down by an angry undercurrent of frustrated reaction. Their emotional body (water sign) is so powerful, so titanic in response, that those around them often feel the "sting" of disappointment and the "lash" of disillusioned revenge. On the other hand, their quiet ways, their endurance and inner control (once their desire nature is contained) make them most valuable in any field where strong leadership is needed in a hidden and conservative way.

With laser beam intensity, these I WANT people will move into a situation, go to the core of the problem and then relentlessly pursue its conclusion. The intensity of desire pushes away all obstacles in their path, like an unrelenting bulldozer plowing through the countryside. They make wonderful detectives.

Physical energy and endurance stand out like beacons of strength when most others will give in or collapse from disappointment or exhaustion. Not so with the I WANT people. They will continually persevere in quiet watchfulness, cautiously hiding the emotional depths of their desire nature.

The I WANT people must learn that when their wishes are not realized, they cannot give way to resentment. Taking offense smolders within like a dangerous growth. They must learn to release the desire and wait for a better time. Patience and foresight are needed here.

The extremism of the I WANT people can swing from an all-consuming materialism to a complete dedication to the highest of spiritual principles. Their emotions are everywhere – high or low. They can NEVER be indifferent! There has to be an aim or ideal to stretch for, or life will not feel complete. Emotional sensitivity may even cause them to become very difficult to live or work with. However, once challenged constructively, they will respond with vigor and determination.

The inner desires that consume them, sometimes beyond their control, need to be calmed with quiet moments of peaceful introspection and meditative understanding. They need to ponder upon the larger mysteries of life in order to unravel some of their own plots and subplots they weave with such emotional force. Remember, the scorpion, in its ultimate anger, has been known to sting itself to death! They need to look upon the greater symbols for Scorpio and take their meanings as examples to follow in their life and actions!

Once the I WANT people are aware of the hidden fire within them – once they have decided they have had enough of the suffering scars of emotional turmoil – once they understand the dangers of possessiveness and too strong a self will – THEN, they can turn that deep sensitivity into a magnificent healing ray of calmness (for themselves and for others). THEN, they can turn that hidden fire of emotion into the deeper spiritual vision of the New Age.

With mystical insight, they can lead us to the heights of human endeavor and into the deepest meanings of life. After all, they do possess the Serpentine wisdom and that soaring ability of the Eagle. These I WANT people can teach us all how to use the creative function of man's will to triumph over all things earthly. Above all, they have the power of the Phoenix Bird to transmute – to change – to transform the difficulties of the human world, be it sickness of the mind or sickness of the body. They are the healers of the Zodiac!

But first, they must heal themselves !

Therefore, go search out the Scorpio type people. Watch them and feel what they are going through. You will learn much and you can assist greatly by being patient and understanding with this intense, sincere vibration.

Remember the scorpion –

the serpent –

the eagle –

and (above all) the Phoenix bird!

Then, remember to appreciate the power and potential glory of this strong vibration.

Scorpio is the second of three WATER signs –
CANCER, SCORPIO & PISCES

SAGITTARIUS

November 22 - December 22

This is the Last of the Three FIRE Signs

Now, the precious rays of the Sun are moving into the sign of Sagittarius, from November 22 to December 22. This vibration is rather an unusual one. We are going into winter here. This is where most of nature starts to go deep within. So with the Sagittarius vibration, the visionary qualities of the human spirit appear from deep within their human soul. They prepare mankind for a gateway to a utopian world.

In the mental world, the Sagittarius type people possess a remarkable binocular ability to "see the big picture" – to grasp the significance of total perspective. Being naturally prophetic, many of them have been born with an uncanny flair to sense the future and foresee results BEFORE they happen. Such qualities make these Sagittarius type people invaluable in any situation where long-range planning is needed. Most Sagittarians dislike being bound by limit or pressured into making decisions. Their free-wheeling attitudes and easy–going manner needs boundless space to flourish, mentally as well as physically. They love the space – the freedom in which to roam and explore, in everything they do. Travel, especially, excites them!

These individuals have a wonderful sense of humor. They exude cheerfulness, enhanced with a rather cosmopolitan innocence. Their delightful humor will help to strengthen friendships, for they never fail to see the foibles of others without some whimsical observation or kindly understanding. Frankness abounds like the refreshing breeze of purified mountain air. Honesty and integrity compose their badge of courage, seeming to always be motivated by high, philanthropic desire.

The Sagittarius type people will think a long time before committing themselves – another keen indication of their ability to "see the big picture". Being extremely active in body as well as mind, they strive for the highest and best in everything they do. They love sports – the lure of the game – the challenge of superior physical strength – the open air and the freedom that comes with it. These are the outdoor type people, moving with giant strides, as if to conquer space. Many walk with a galloping gait, impatient to get going. Their restlessness for adventure and travel dominate their strong need for independence.

It is best to describe this unusual Sagittarian vibration as the "musketeer" of the 21st century. They so exemplify the gallant fighter – so swashbuckling and grandiose in manner. They will fight for the right for each individual to have his space. They are perpetual students, forever learning as the life experience itself becomes an unending classroom for them. They observe everything – taking the long view to sense and "see" the future trends with the diligence of a scholar and the humanity of a philosopher.

THE CENTAUR

(Seek the Essence of this Sign)

The pictograph for the Sagittarius has always been the Centaur – half man and half beast. By now, I am sure you realize these pictographs for the signs of the Zodiac have not been designed by chance. There always is a deep significance between the pictograph and the sign it represents. Indeed, a picture is worth a thousand words!

The Centaur symbolically serves a two-fold purpose:

The upper half is pictured as a man with a bow and arrow aimed for the stars. This is a very significant symbol for the Sagittarius type people. Within them, they have a powerful urge to reach for man's highest achievements, especially in the realm of philosophy. With sure aim, they desire to shoot the arrow to its mark with swift action and absolute decision. They see the future with insight that borders on the prophetic. They travel rapidly, whether in physical movement or mental journey – seeking adventure and truth. This is their "modus operandi". In Greek legend, the Centaurs were respected as

wise men. They were often the **teachers** of the great, young heroes of mythology.

The lower half is pictured as a beast-like creature of great strength. This symbolically indicates an attachment to the physical world of sports and physical achievement. Many fine athletes have a strong Sagittarian influence in their natal chart, be it the Sun or any other planet. Wanting to be the "best" – to raise their standard to its finest – is always their earnest desire. The example of the Olympic Games exemplifies the criterion for their high standards. The Sagittarius type people also love the challenge of the game.

The Centaur was the philosopher teacher of old. Today, the symbolism continues the parallel. At any time, you will find these Sagittarius type people gravitating toward the areas of philosophy, metaphysics, distant travel and foreign adventure. Many of them will be involved in philanthropic works.

As you observe them, you will find their minds to be quick, able to grasp the essentials of a problem and synthesize it into an understandable whole. They possess an extraordinary ability to explain matters clearly to others, especially those who seem to be sinking into an emotional quagmire or vacillating with indecision. Philosophical strains are woven into all they think as they have the potential to become the masters of positive thought!

The most harmful thing one can do to these Sagittarius type people is to limit their freedom, be it physical or mental. Like 'bulls in the china shop', they will feel misplaced or become rebellious. Restraint only produces utter frustration – similar to a race horse locked into his gate at the opening of his race. It is only by allowing the wisdom of their introspection to flow – to touch the spiritual plane of thought – that they will be able to "see", with clarity. It is then they will understand the essential spirituality of each individual and their importance in life. They do possess visionary qualities that the world so needs!

Being a fire sign, they also possess natural leadership tendencies. At times, with fiery impetuosity and risking danger, they will work to maintain a hero's posture. They can inspire others with hope and vision. They continually sound the call for inner freedom, enjoying the challenge of each day with resourceful spirit. Indeed, they instinctively understand that every experience in life is filled with the potential for growth – filled with the promise of intoxicating action and stimulating thought.

The Keywords for Sagittarius

I SEE

The Sagittarius type people usually have conversations laced with "I can see your point" or "Do you see what I mean?" or "Is it clear to you ?" Their hunches are predictive, sagacious and prudent. In other words, you can trust them. Think of the lyrics of the song – "On a clear day you can see forever". Well, the Sagittarian vibration, at times, actually can! If you observe them in a contemplative manner, you will notice their gaze to be remote, cloaked in deep thought – like joggers gauging their distance and speed. Then, as they share their thoughts and ideas, you will marvel at their ability to see "the big picture".

The I SEE people have a magic all their own! It comes with the ability to SEE into problems and visualize the outcomes. They take the time to check the overview before becoming committed. They seem to have the knack of looking at situations in a total, philosophical way before saying anything. With effortless ease and uncomplicated directedness, they can and do inspire confidence in their judgment.

Since freedom is so important to them, they call "home" wherever they hang their hat. They possess an easy adaptability to enjoy life to its fullest, whatever or wherever the circumstances. Again, this goes back to their basic philosophical nature and the tremendous reserve of wisdom they seem to tap into with their I SEE attitude.

Generally active and restless, the I SEE people revolt inwardly, as well as verbally against any sort of discipline or restriction. At times, even concentration is difficult despite their large capacity for learning. They will need to cultivate the determination to finish what they have started with the same enthusiasm and vigor of the initial spurt of energy they began with.

Regarding knowledge, the I SEE people have an insatiable appetite for it – observing and learning wherever they are. Their gregarious nature and fun sense of humor – their free and open manner – places their special vibration in the category of "sterling friendship". The wit is quick and frank. They penetrate idiosyncrasies with incisive marksmanship and yet tickle the funny bone at the same time.

The I SEE people seem to have this insistent urge within them to SEE the truth and to utilize this knowledge with positive thought and action. We consider them to be champions of human endeavor. We see them as guardians of the universal principles that civilize our planet!

Inner Vision is a special gift for these I SEE people. They seem to be able to gauge a man's abilities – to SEE ahead, unobstructed, and clear-headed. They seem to function in a world that cries for peace and justice. It is the expansive Jupiter vibration (its ruling planet) through osmosis that can lift materialistic thought and encourage philanthropic work. Indeed, the spirit within must be unencumbered. The call of adventure does weave the fabric of their life style – be it a trip across town or a distant safari. But always, they are seeking to understand – to be illuminated with true wisdom.

Hats off to the I SEE people !! They lead the way to greater vision of a better world. The most delightful part of this vision is the refreshing wit, the penetrating insight and the free and pleasant manner in which they move.

The rest of the Zodiac family can learn much here.
★Tip your hat, with a smile, to the I SEE people!

★Shake their hand and feel the comradery!

★Love the essence of them for their giving, open nature!

★Laugh with them as you sense their comic flair and heady laughter!

Sagittarius is the last of the three FIRE Signs –
ARIES, LEO & SAGITTARIUS

CAPRICORN

♑

December 22 – January 21

This is the third and last of the EARTH signs

The Capricorn vibration is one of the most difficult of the Zodiacal signs to understand. Perhaps, if we watch, as the winter season begins, we will find nature preparing for its harshness. This is part of the qualities of this sign. This is the season where winter takes hold. Every animal must now use common sense and plan as well as they can to prepare for a long winter. Has it ever occurred to you that they must do so with diligence and forethought? So it is with the Capricorn type people.

This earth sign signals the necessity to prepare and plan for life. Actually, it does seem incomprehensible to others that these people WANT to plan and work. Indeed, they do so with diligent endeavor. The Capricorn type people seem to have been born with the mentality of enduring work, and loving it! It is almost as if they are driven to succeed – mindless of the hours, days or even years it may take to bring the desired success.

To the Capricorn type people, whether your Sun in this time span or any other planet(s) are placed in it – you have come into this world with the capacity to endure a great deal of hardship and the self discipline to insure the fulfillment of your ambition. There are times when they do come across as stuffy, uptight, very proper or quite reserved. But, they do have the built-in understanding for the right time, the right place and the right action! Their minds cipher like computer channels, building fact upon fact. They deal only with reality as they see it. Practical needs are uppermost in their mind, weighing the usefulness of anything or anyone in their lives. Calculation and equitable judgment are their strongest points.

Not given to open displays of emotion, they can be quite standoffish and reserved. At times, they may even seem unapproachable. Dignity marks their carriage and they manifest a powerful sense of propriety. However, if you look deeply beyond this exterior, you will find conscientious and shy individuals who really want to accomplish the fair and just thing.

The Capricorn type people have a will power that is all pervading. It is not like the will power of the intrepid Leo or the dominant Taurus. It is a will power interwoven with iron discipline and a factual approach. Governmental work and political considerations are strong. Many may work within the confines of government, as civil servants or as organizers in political organizations. They are very concerned about law and order. They possess a strong conservative outlook from their "lookout tower" and tend to gravitate toward management, teaching, or any field where disciplined administration is essential. They make very hardheaded and practical business people.

Perhaps one of their most outstanding characteristics is their essential ability to be methodical and reliable. Their determination and independence allows them to achieve any objective they set out to accomplish (regardless of how overpowering or difficult the obstacles). The amazing thing about the Capricorn type people is that they ANTICIPATE setbacks and NEVER underestimate the magnitude of any undertaking. With a deep breath and intense "gathering of energy", they will begin **any** effort with determined patience.

This one-pointedness with which they approach life, coupled with the ability to make extensive sacrifices to achieve, puts them at the top of the list for accomplishment! They are the people who GET things done!

THE GOAT

(Seek the Essence of This Sign)

The symbol of the Goat bears a great deal of thought here for there is much similarity to the qualities and habits of the Capricorn type people. The Goat is a hardy animal that moves with sure-footedness, especially on those high, craggy climbs and stony paths. The Goat ascends hills and mountains with determination and patient effort – never quitting until the top is reached. They climb to an area where no other can venture except a winged brother. This sign also rules the knees, the part of the body so necessary to climb with. (It is also necessary to kneel with – some call it humility!)

Goats live frugally, eating whatever is available and keeping pretty much to themselves. There is a strong similarity here to the Capricorn vibration. The traits seem quite comparable. You will find them desiring to reach the summit of whatever they choose with a similar ambition and persistence. They attempt to climb the ladder of success with the same effort and dogged determination of the Goat. Capricorn type people know full well that discipline and austerity are the necessary "tools" for attainment.

They can be serious and melancholic to a fault. Perhaps, when you learn this about them, you will be able to help them laugh at themselves and their foibles, rather than become depressed. Melancholy is like a second skin. The burden of responsibility lies heavily upon them. How they so need to learn how to laugh and enjoy the little moments of merriment. How they so need to appreciate the family and cultivate a deep sense of brotherhood – over and beyond material achievement.

Respect is a fundamental element for them. With dignified and proper ways, they **can** appear uncompromising at times; stern taskmasters who cannot "seem" to understand. Actually, they feel they are quite just in their decisions. Facts are facts. They relate intimately with the common sense of daily living. Practical and material issues are paramount on their scale of judgment. They realize the limitations of the physical. Still, if anything is not based on fact, then it has no use for them.

Their concentration is remarkable. So is their fortitude. However, they must be careful they do not place too much emphasis on the "material life", but more on the "substance of the spirit". This can be facilitated by their deep love and kinship with nature. Inner peace flows easily to them when they witness a beautiful pastoral scene or become absorbed with fine music. They do realize beauty is necessary for them in life!

As a hardy Goat climbs and controls the dangerous cliffs, so do the Capricorn type people look to success as the ultimate perch in life. A haunting fear can pervade their efforts if they feel unfulfilled in whatever they desire to achieve. They welcome responsibility, possessing an administrator's eye for efficient performance. Perhaps, more than any other sign, these individuals do indicate a willingness to pay the price for success. They seem to give devotion and hard work precedence over anything else. However, we must never forget they do radiate the teacher–philosopher vibration with their serious nature and love of history. Their lessons of the past are never forgotten and hardly ever repeated. They learn well! Certainly, they do inspire others with the lessons of discipline and dedication, surpassed by no other Zodiacal sign.

The Keywords for Capricorn

I USE

You must now understand how their keywords, I USE, are fitting for such an earth sign. Remember, the Capricorn type people soundly comprehend the value of earthly possessions and their use. The I USE people see through the eyes of a pragmatist. If anything or anyone is useful or practical, then it is viewed as good. These key words, I USE, are often sprinkled throughout their conversations.

The I USE people weigh, judge, decide and utilize only in the light of active service. Their strong inclination is practicality! If it does not work, they discard it quickly and move on to something else that will. Their ingenuity and adaptability to make things work for their benefit is uncanny. But, remember, the I USE mentality is like the trusty "kitchen apron". It is one where work and accomplishment is implicitly applied. Always, there must be a purpose and use to everything they say, do, think and create. Even though they love beauty and strive to own precious things, they, too, must have a USEFUL purpose or value.

Capricorn type people are active people! They are the doers who get things done efficiently, with minimum effort. Perhaps you may not like their methods – serious, determined and (unfortunately) sometimes ruthless – but they DO GET THINGS DONE! According to them, law and order are the "nuts and bolts" that keep this civilized world together. To them, a rule is a rule and must be kept.

Yet, on the other hand, they possess astounding "prudence" as their common sense demands that only intelligent action flow at all times. They may appear reticent, reserved, shy or plain introverted – but this is a cover up for a realistic, down-to-earth, and cautious, nature that percolates deep within.

It has often been said that the Capricorn type people, when they appear young, have an adult approach – an "old head on young shoulders". This expression denotes the sobriety of this sign. Their childhood is generally difficult as they feel responsibility keenly. However, as they grow older, they do gain in wisdom, for life gets better as they get older.

With every passing year, they learn from experience and gain wisdom in bits and pieces. If ever hurt deeply, they will never make the same mistake again. Indeed, the lessons of life do fall on fertile ground for them. The I USE people mellow with age. As they get older, it does get better. Perhaps it is because they are finally able to comprehend the intricacies of life experiences with their ever ready, astute, common sense approach!

There are times when the I USE people feel very alone! This is the time to develop a sense of humor and learn how to relax.

They soon will learn that the drive for achievement is hollow if there is not some joy in life. They so need a little consideration! You can help these conscientious people with gentle compliments and occasional praise. That they will accept!

At times, they work SO hard and feel SO unappreciated. Perhaps this is the reason for their often cited melancholia. Never forget the gifts they bring to your world – the gift of common sense – the gift of being useful and sensible – the gift of the need for law and order – and above all, the gift of the serious, practical approach to individual freedom. The I USE people do send out into the world the structured resonances everyone can USE. Indeed, where would we be without such a practical, down-to-earth vibration?

★They possess the qualities of reliability –prudence – patience – efficiency!

★They guide us in the need for practical living.

★They teach us an ambitious drive to succeed.

The wisdom, as they age, grows to where they finally know how to "smell the roses".

Common sense – cool heads – perseverance – achievement.

Go find some hardy Capricorn people. You can learn much from them.

Capricorn is the last of the EARTH signs –
TAURUS, VIRGO & CAPRICORN

AQUARIUS

January 21 – February 19

This is the Last of the Three AIR Signs

Anyone born between January 21st to February 19th has a dominant Aquarian vibration. This includes anyone born with planet(s) in the sign of Aquarius.

Of all the sign qualities, Aquarian type people represent the eternal manifestation of true brotherly love in the simple way they express their feelings and actions. Respect for each individual is of the highest importance to them. They truly understand the drive for inner freedom as well as the vital need for outer freedom. They instinctively allow you the right to be as you are and to whatever stage in life you are connected to, at any given time.

Equality and fraternity are their code words. These words trigger open a reservoir of human understanding that is not duplicated in any other sign.

Working with people and interacting with human need is important to them. Perhaps the most striking observation I have witnessed with this vibration is the detachment they usually have in approaching any situation. This detachment is as impersonal as a telephone pole on a deserted highway! They possess an aloofness that seems almost dispassionate and cold although they do appear friendly and kindly in nature. DO NOT BE MISLED! They are not cold people – even though they may **appear** this way. It is only because they have the ability to divorce their emotions from their cool analysis of the situations at hand. As a result, the personal in their lives become somewhat limited in expression. Thus, it is easy to misunderstand the Aquarian type people in personal relationships due to this seemingly indifferent manner. Remember, beneath their exterior beats a heart overflowing with love and emotion. They are very passionate in a most seemingly "dispassionate" way.

They are friendly, outgoing, independent, idealistic and, unconventional. They also can be unyielding, once their mind is made up. Very progressive in nature, they are attuned to modern advancement including scientific discoveries and the proliferation of inventions.

They are very aware of the evolving vibrations that constantly flood the earth plane. This gives them the ability to have ideas and inventions years ahead of their time. Thomas Edison was a great Aquarian example of this. His progressive and forward thinking brought much benefit to mankind. Sometimes, the Aquarian type people can be looked upon as eccentric or marching to their own tune because of their advanced creativity.

The sciences, the exploration of the universe, metaphysics and New Age subjects lead their mind to the untapped and endless possibilities within and without the universe – it fascinates them! Indeed, their natural intuition and scientific bent could combine to allow them to become very fine astrologers.

THE WATER BEARER

(Seek the Essence of this Sign)

The pictograph for the sign of Aquarius is that of a human figure pouring from an urn. Although this pictograph has been called the "water bearer", symbolically, it is NOT water being poured out but WISDOM of the intuitive nature! Perhaps, Wisdom Bearer would have been a more appropriate name.

Those prone to a strong Aquarian vibration will relate to this symbol. Their intuitive faculties constantly flow into brilliant strains of original thought. They can tune into knowing in a flash – and yet not knowing how or why – but KNOWING!! With unexpected, lightening force, illuminative ideas shake their slumbering consciousness with the brilliance of thought and incisive speed. This is the dynamic, intuitive ability of the Aquarian type people.

The pictograph of the Water Bearer has been connected to the Age of Aquarius, which has just begun. It will be a long trek through the centuries of the next 2000 years. Such an Age foretells the establishment of brotherly love as the norm for human relationships, and raising the consciousness of mankind to a higher spiritual and humanitarian level of peace and brotherhood. Edgar Cayce, the great sleeping prophet of the 20th century called it the "time of 1000 years of peace and brotherhood".

It is a long process, this awakening of the higher consciousness. It is a long process to bring every human being on earth to the actuality of a more harmonious world – dedicated to the living concept of brotherhood. Actually, the basis of the Aquarian Age is " loving your neighbor as yourself".

The Aquarian nature intuitively KNOWS this is possible! It can be done! The Aquarian type people are well fitted to this pictograph. Seemingly detached from the emotional quandary most others find themselves in, they seem to be able to operate with better objectivity. Their intuitive forces can register without hypersensitive reaction. These are times when they can appear to be cold and insensitive. Do not believe this! What they have is the ability to divorce themselves from turmoil – an ability that may seem indifferent to others – but they do care deeply within.

At some point, in the lives of the Aquarian type people, the stimulus of the vibrations from the Planet Uranus (the ruler of Aquarius) will move (with striking speed) to awaken their minds to the "awareness" of the spiritual laws that govern life. Perhaps this is why the Aquarian type people love so deeply and yet at a distance.

Instinctively, the Aquarian type people realize the "importance" of the individual and how necessary it is for others to have the freedom to be themselves. Given to extremes, the Aquarian type people can be looked upon as different or odd. They march to a different drummer! They do not seem to mind. They are so strongly individual they can withstand any type of peer pressure.

Kindly as they are, they can become veritable walls of toughness and determination when they believe in what they do. They KNOW they are committed to what they do – a knowing that comes from deep within. No one can shake it. Many do not even understand it. It is part and parcel of their very soul commitment – this knowing!

The Keywords for Aquarius

I KNOW

The I KNOW keywords for Aquarius are powerful. With these words comes a quiet, insistent power that they are in command on a different level of thought. Remember, this is an air sign – the quality of the mind. Gemini deals with the conscious mind. Libra deals with the subconscious mind. But the Aquarian deals with the super conscious mind. This is the area where intuition takes precendence. As we approach the end of the astrological signs, we are now moving into areas not usually ventured into. It is the higher, spiritual mode – like the tendrils of a hardy plant, searching for the light. Here, the Aquarian nature, once awakened, moves into the intuitive stage of knowing – the guide to his successful approach to life.

When in conversation with Aquarian type people, you will become very aware of their keywords I KNOW. This understanding of the I KNOW percolates throughout their conversation like generously sprinkled spice. They punctuate with decisive emphasis on points they wish to express. They JUST know! Their intuition is constantly tumbling forth with certainty. The super conscious mind is in full bloom!

Sometimes, the seeming "arrogance" of these key words may often trigger perplexity or frustration from others. Try to understand the true Aquarian nature. They do not intend to be abrupt or discourteous or flippant. They REALLY DO KNOW! Knowledge and understanding flows through them in flashes. It is instinctive and they themselves, many times, are unaware of how or why they KNOW – but they do know!

They dwell on a mental plane, in a world of ideas and ideals. Injustice and inequality, to others as well as themselves, sears them with indignation. It is incomprehensible to them to see others treated with callousness or indifference. Their humanitarian nature guides them in the knowledge that everyone must be free to be themselves.

They possess a down-to-earth realism when dealing with others. They do not expect much. They have this admirable quality of accepting people as they are. Because of this quality, they get along quite well with their companions; becoming loyal and trusted friends. In fact, to the Aquarius type people, friendship means everything! If you are married to an Aquarian type person, you need to be a friend first! AND if you cannot accept their friends, BEWARE for their friends are as precious as family!

As they mature with life experience, these ideals of freedom and brotherhood will manifest into concrete action. Be it the Hall of Fame or difficulty with the law – there is a vast range of extremism, as well as independence, that courses through them. In their desire for freedom, their brilliance of thought and inventive genius can uplift and aid humanity. On the other hand, this desire for freedom, at all cost, if not realistic, can explode beyond the bounds of society and alienate others. They cannot be a law unto themselves!

The I KNOW people dislike hypocrisy and artificiality. They desire real people and seek companionship on all levels. Their friends are all important! Their life approach is people! The I KNOW quality understands that only by cooperating with others and assisting others can true happiness be found. This intuitive nature works best in organizational situations. Although they can be tireless workers, they need the freedom to be independent in thought and action. Then you will see the "fruits" of their labor blossom.

Where would we be without the needed special energy the I KNOW people send out?

Where would you find such fine examples for humanitarian effort and expanding consciousness?

Who would constantly keep you attuned to the right of everyone to radiate to their true self?

These are the vibrations the I KNOW people pour forth.

★They transmit the precious need for achieving the goals and aims of the Aquarian Age – inalienable right to "life, liberty and the pursuit of happiness".

★These are the vibrations of the I KNOW people as they cut the rugged path into the future with boldness – clear vision – and the promise of the reality of peace and common brotherhood !

★These are the "Tillers of mankind" tending to the seed of loving "thy neighbor as thyself". The **I KNOW** people know this already!

Therefore, go search out the Aquarius type people – watch them – understand their great potential and LOVE them for it!

Aquarius is the last of the three AIR signs –
GEMINI, LIBRA & AQUARIUS

PISCES

♓

February 20 – March 21

This is the last of the three Water Signs

The Piscean vibration is perhaps the most mystifying of all the Zodiacal signs. This is the period, just before Spring, when all of nature's energies are gathering in a hidden, subtle way to prepare for the growing season. This is the period from February 20 to March 21. Similarly, the Pisces type people are influenced by their surroundings in the same subtle manner. This is due to their extreme sensitivity to the needs and emotional responses of themselves as well as of others. There are times when their emotional needs so overwhelm them that tears or moods of frustration are often too close to the surface.

It seems that many Pisces type people have some condition in their lives that appears to limit their expansion. They are, perhaps, the most creative of all the Zodiacal signs. They can ascend to the heights of creativity easily. Generally speaking, they are kind, gentle and tender souls. They radiate a "velvet warmth" that soothes like a comforting blanket, woven with love and concern. Their compassion knows no bounds! Being the true "sensors" of the Zodiac, they are responsive to every nuance or suggestion filtering through the human family.

Inner peace is what they seek, whether consciously or not. Sometimes, they will need to withdraw to maintain their equilibrium. Possessing a soft and thoughtful manner, they can be the gentle friend to lean on – the willing shoulder to cry on. Their look, their understanding, their open heart, their insight bordering on the profound – are great comforts to the less fortunate in every way. As a result of this ability, many Piscean type people will seek employment in fields such as medicine, nursing, the healing arts, teaching and any such similar profession that cares for others.

However, at various points in their lives, the outside world may appear harsh and unyielding. In order to preserve their delicate balance, they may need to retreat into periods of solitude and calm. Sleep can be most beneficial for their sensitive nature, but, unfortunately, it also can be an escape from facing reality. In their desire to seek relief from the pressures of a coarse world, they must be careful not to seek comfort in any "escapist" method that helps elude the harshness of the moment. Anything that clouds their reasoning is dangerous – whether it is habitual day dreaming, alcohol, gambling, tobacco, and especially, drugs. If you feel any similarity to these tendencies, then perhaps you have a strong Piscean strain within you. Check your planetary placements.

The Piscean nature is most delicate and beautiful. Their giving nature and trusting ways need special understanding. Piscean children are most delicate to raise. They need special understanding and enormous amounts of patience, especially when they dissolve in tears through utter frustration. However, the rewards of patient parental effort will bring much consideration and appreciation from this precious, gentle vibration.

You can help the Piscean type people immensely by being **considerate** to their moods and sensitive nature. They are mirroring what is around them! I often think of the delicacy of velvet. When rubbed the wrong way, it disturbs the beauty of the fabric and its glow – but when pressed smoothly, the right way, you can appreciate the sheen and softness of its beauty and velvet nature. So it is with the Piscean vibration. Treat them with some of the consideration they shower upon others so willingly. Then, witness the finest in faithful love and tender devotion.

THE FISH

(Seek the essence of this sign)

The pictograph for this sign of Pisces has always seemed paradoxical to me – the picture of two fish swimming in opposite directions. Within the Piscean vibration, there is a strong connection to this pictograph. The fact that they are swimming in opposite directions indicates the strong duality of this sign. One fish, symbolically, is swimming into the mainstream of life, the real, practical world – the other fish, symbolically, is swimming in the opposite direction, filled with the potential of the transcendental awareness of the oneness of life – the Universal force that pulsates throughout creation. This duality is so much a part of them.

Emotion, being synonymous with water, is the basis for many individuals with strong Piscean vibrations. They are the "soul" of emotion and feeling. Their sensitivity knows no bounds.

★When someone cries, they feel the pain!
★ When someone is lost, they feel the fear!
★When someone is in turmoil or despair, they feel the hopelessness!

They are the most sensitive of all the signs of the Zodiac. They are natural "mediums" tapping the inner, psychic world with ease.

This may seem incomprehensible to those of you who are completely interwoven in the practical aspects of life. However, if you pause to consider the two fish and their opposite directions, perhaps you will be able to comprehend the fluidity of the Piscean nature.

The first fish, swimming into the main stream of life is filled with fear, anxiety and longing for secure protection. It seeks relief from the responsibilities that seem to "choke" it.

The second fish, swimming in the opposite direction, is filled with the potential of the transcendental awareness of the oneness of life – The Universal Force that pulsates throughout creation.

This duality helps them endure their existence and yet, long for freedom, expansion, and no painful emotional attachments. Their dreams and visions are the lifelines that help them tolerate their sensitive life. It can even elevate them beyond everyday living into the spiritual qualities that mark their unique psychic gifts. They also need, at times, to accept the conditions surrounding them with patience and strong faith.

Remember, you are dealing with the MOST sensitive vibration of the Zodiac. They feel other people's pain and sadness, as if it were their own. They absorb the thoughts and emotional states of others easily. Sometimes they believe it is their own thoughts and own emotional states. Such is the vulnerability and heightened sensitivity of these gentle souls.

The Pisces type people are extremely gifted, especially in the field of music. They have an impressionable, responsive nature that produces fine artists in every cultural field. They are tender, romantic and thoughtful. Perhaps their greatest lesson is to "control their thoughts" and tune into their own inner guidance!

There will also be times when they will sorely need solitude to catch their breath from the frantic merry-go-round of daily activity. Once recharged, they will be ready to move again, amid the fierceness of life's competitive ways. However, please remember, they will always move with the healing balm of gentle love and generous compassion.

The Keywords for Pisces

I BELIEVE

If you are familiar with the Pisces type people, you will find the keywords, I BELIEVE a prerequisite to any conversation they have. "I believe" or "I can believe it" or "It's unbelievable" are the keywords that consistently tell you about themselves. Believing is a childlike, trusting quality. It implies faith of the finest degree. It is a knowing that transcends the physical limitations. It goes beyond the earthly connections to the very spiritual essence of humanity. Faith in the Universal Source and faith in YOU is their most powerful inspirational quality.

On the other hand, the I BELIEVE people can be influenced by negativity. They will need to learn how to control their fluctuating thoughts and restless imagination. Unknown fears may nag at them. Many times, unwittingly, they pick up the dark and fearful conditions that surround them and their environment. Being the natural psychics of the Zodiac, they possess an instinctive awareness of the interacting vibrations of others. They are very responsive to every nuance. When things get tough, they may seek escape. Beware of drugs, alcohol or any such stimulant that dulls the senses. It can be dangerous for such a delicate nature. Such things can entrap them into a life filled with pain and escapism.

Perhaps, the most frustrating part for the I BELIEVE people is their ability to be overly optimistic on one hand and pessimistic on the other. They are keenly aware of the duality of their nature. This "seesaw" condition creates waves of discontent and unhappiness. The I BELIEVE people can sometimes get lost in the ensuing surges of hopelessness that wash over them in difficult times.

The I BELIEVE people are not combative or aggressive by nature. They prefer to deal on the gentle, nurturing levels. They would rather suffer injury than fight for their rights. An element of sacrifice is usually dominant in their nature and they will suffer in silence or heartbreak when they feel lonely and misunderstood. They want so much to do the right thing! The great solvent for them is consideration from those around them.

It is quite easy to dominate the gentle Piscean nature by forcing feelings of guilt upon them. Their intense desire to serve and be helpful opens their trusting nature to unscrupulous individuals who can take advantage of their high ideals and willingness to help. They MUST be constantly wary of those who try to make them FEEL guilty! Such unwarranted guilt feelings can result in emotional slavery!

Help the I BELIEVE people to stand apart and face the future with the tremendous faith they do possess within themselves.

Help them realize the power and the radiating effects of the healing they send forth with their kindly, unselfish and devoted ways.

Help them end that timidity and anxiety that haunts their thoughts and limits their actions.

Help them find that inner peace, they so long for, with your own kindness. They give so much to others.

To the final, and most inspiring of ALL the twelve signs of the Zodiac – never forget what the I BELIEVE people bring into this world:

★The ultimate in self sacrifice –

★The spiritual in that eternal search for peace and happiness

★The consummate in human understanding and compassion!!

Go find some Piscean type people and listen to them! Return a little of their great unselfishness! Love them for their gentle kind ways! The Last and final sign of the Zodiac is the giving, loving Pisces! They are the LINK to our greater world of unselfish love and true compassion!

PISCES is the last of the three WATER Signs –
CANCER, SCORPIO & PISCES

NOTE WELL:

This is the first step in understanding the characteristics of all the twelve signs of the Zodiac. Hopefully, you have grasped the essence of each sign. Now, watch the actions and reactions of yourself, and others you know, who are born in the same or different Sun-sign, according to their birthday. You see how you and they will continually radiate to the power of the Sun and the sign it is in at birth.

Moreover, I trust you will begin to realize (as you read further) how INDISPENSABLE the qualities of each sign are to the development of every individual (beyond the Sun-Sign). There will be a zodiacal sign on the cusp of each of the twelve houses of your natal chart. All these signs contribute to your developing as a total individual.

Where would you be without the optimism and drive of the Aries or the practical stability of the Taurus?

Where would you be without the communications system of the inquisitive Gemini or the home-loving, sustaining instincts of the Cancer?

Would life have its zest and sparkle without the loving, dramatic Leo or a meaningful existence without the dedication and service of the Virgo?

Could you negotiate fairly without the balancing of the Libra or strive to understand the mysteries of life and death without the probings of the intense Scorpio?

Would you stumble in the darkness without the foresight and wisdom of the Sagittarius or accomplish anything of worth without the dedication and discipline of the Capricorn?

Finally, how could you ever hope to achieve any sort of humanitarian value or philosophy without the illuminative powers of Aquarius or feel the compassion and gentle receptivity of the Pisces?

Can you see how each sign brings with it the necessary qualities every human being **needs** in order to develop into a balanced and harmonious individual?

The vastness of this subject and its interpretations are endless and wondrous. Here is a body of knowledge that is as deep and fulfilling as its interpreter. You have only begun the basics of this knowledge, with the description of each Zodiacal sign.

The great planets, and their unique planetary patterns were designed to send you revealing messages – guiding you toward the fulfillment of the greatness within. With chart in hand and compassion in heart, the astrologer is simply the messenger trying to help you UNDERSTAND and see ahead!

CHAPTER THREE

THE SIGNS of the ZODIAC by ELEMENTS :

FIRE
AIR
EARTH
WATER

Sun-Sign Compatibility-

Is there such a Possibility?

The ASTROLOGICAL SIGNS
by

The ELEMENTS -
(also called the Triplicities)
Fire Air, Earth and Water

THE ELEMENTS

There are three signs for each element – that is why it is called a triplicity.

Each group represents HARMONY within the ELEMENT.

Fire Element: Aries, Leo & Sagittarius
ALL three FIRE signs are compatible.

Air Element: Gemini, Libra & Aquarius
ALL three AIR signs are compatible.

Earth Element: Taurus, Virgo & Capricorn
ALL three EARTH signs are compatible.

Water Element: Cancer, Scorpio & Pisces
ALL three WATER signs are compatible.

FIRE needs AIR to Ignite and Burn –
All FIRE and AIR signs are compatible.

EARTH needs WATER to grow Vegetation –
All EARTH and WATER signs are compatible.

Now, let's examine it from a metaphysical point of view:

FIRE Signs

The FIRE element represents the SPIRIT – the immortal seed within you.

ARIES describes your spiritual connection with the God force. Keyword: I AM

LEO describes the spiritual connection within your Heart.
Keyword: I WILL

SAGITTARIUS describes the spiritual vision of humanity.
Keyword: I SEE

AIR Signs

The AIR element represents the MIND – your thinking, reasoning nature.

GEMINI describes the conscious use of the instinctive mind.
Keyword: I THINK

LIBRA describes the subconscious mind of righteous living.
Keyword: I BALANCE

AQUARIUS describes the intuitive superconscious mind.
Keyword: I KNOW

WATER Signs

The WATER element represents the EMOTION – your soul capacity to feel.

CANCER describes the conscious soul – feeling emotion.
Keyword: I FEEL

SCORPIO describes the critical soul – examining emotion.
Keyword: I WANT

PISCES describes the emotional soul – living the emotion.
Keyword: I BELIEVE

EARTH Signs

The EARTH element represents the BODY – the physical being.

TAURUS describes the physical body – attached to earth.
Keyword: I HAVE

VIRGO describes the analytical body – treasuring earth.
Keyword: I ANALYZE

CAPRICORN describes the practical body – functioning well.
Keyword: I USE

The metaphysical approach encompasses all the signs as we move through life:

As the Spirit moves through you (the fire signs) –
it inspires the Mind (the air signs) –
stimulates the Emotion (the water signs) –
and challenges the Human Body (the earth signs).

ALL functioning on the earth plane as one complex human being!

Now, you can begin to realize how these elements function in your life plan as well as how they apply to others in your life? (For further information read the chapters on Houses and Aspects)

IS THERE SUCH A THING AS SUN-SIGN COMPATIBILITY?

Yes – Through the Understanding The Elements: Fire, Earth Air and Water

As an astrologer, I am frequently asked if a certain Sun-Sign is compatible with another Sun-Sign. To use your Sun-Sign as a basis for comparing the various energy interactions between people would be a great disservice to the subject of astrology and to your own common sense. During the past century, Alan Leo (a most astute English astrologer) tried to inform the reading public by using the Sun-Signs of the Zodiac. It was a great idea. However, since then, Sun-Sign astrology has been misused, abused and misunderstood.

Since every human being is a varied, interwoven mixture of vibrations – since your traits and instincts create a myriad of color and design – how can one Sun-sign tell the whole story?

Only a total comparison of the two charts in questions and an analysis of ALL planets, signs and house placements will produce an intelligent answer!

To Reiterate:

All FIRE Sun-signs are compatible with other FIRE Sun-signs as well as all AIR sun-signs.

All AIR signs are compatible with other AIR signs as well as all FIRE signs.

All WATER Sun-signs are compatible with other WATER Sun-signs as well as all EARTH sun- signs

All EARTH Sun-signs are compatible with other EARTH Sun-signs as well as all WATER sun-signs.

Remember, we are dealing ONLY with the SUN-SIGN – the sign of your SUN at the time of your birth. When you think of the elements, you have to remember the symbolism.

For example, if you want to know if the Gemini Sun-sign (air) is compatible with a Leo Sun-sign (fire). THINK ELEMENTS. You cannot have fire without air!

Now let's take elements that are not compatible. The Aries Sun-sign (fire) is not compatible with a Cancer Sun-sign (water)! THINK ELEMENTS. Water puts out the fire!

These signs tend to be inharmonious because of the nature of the elements, NOT people!

Elements are simple but people are complex!

For example, let's say you are an Aries Sun-Sign (fire) married to a Cancerian Sun-Sign (water). Although the Sun-Signs are incompatible by element (water and fire do not blend), there may well be OTHER PLANETS in very compatible signs (other than their Sun-Signs) in their charts.

For example: In the Aries (fire) chart – compatibility will be there if the Aries person has other planets in water or earth signs from birth. These will harmonize easily with the sensitivity of the Cancerian chart.

Futhermore: In the Cancer (water) chart – compatibility will be there if the Cancer person has other planets in fire or air. These will harmonize easily with the fire of the Aries chart.

So, you see, simple Sun-Sign astrology does not give an accurate and full picture of two individuals. Sun-sign comparison ALONE is INCOMPLETE!

The two astrological charts must be compared in a variety of ways!.

★The Element of the Sun-Sign is ONE of many factors in comparison of two people.

★Elements are only a small part of a very BIG picture.
★In justice, no one can say a marriage, partnership or friendship is or is not workable because of a Sun-sign comparison ALONE.

ONLY the comparison of all the parts of the natal charts of two people in question can provide a comprehensive and accurate study of the interacting energies of each one and their resultant effect upon each other. Comparing two natal charts is a most individual and creative effort!

Many times, a comparison analysis will go a long way in helping each of the parties involved to better understand how they affect each other (and how to adjust and assist each other)! Your uniqueness as an individual can never be fully understood by a Sun-sign description only. Life is too complicated for such simplicity. There are no magical answers either. Unfortunately, the common understanding of astrology is filled with such misconceptions.

There are ten planetary vibrations you radiate to, and the Sun-Sign is only ONE. Although it is the most powerful one, there are still nine other planetary vibrations to consider. Many a troubled relationship can be **aided** with a complete analysis of ALL the "energy patterns" explained fully. You can often be **misled** with the half truths of Sun-Sign interpretation, alone.

Please remember: no relationship, however poor, is hopeless!

Once you compare your energy flows with those of another, you will have given yourself a greater chance to understand the differences as well as the compatibilities.

A heartfelt suggestion:

Being aware of the differences between two people can go a long way toward developing tolerance, understanding and solution.

The Keywords and Essence of the Twelve Signs of the Zodiac

I AM	pioneer	Aries
I HAVE	practicality	Taurus
I THINK	communicator	Gemini
I FEEL	home base	Cancer
I WILL	creative expression	Leo
I ANALYZE	work & health	Virgo
I BALANCE	relationships	Libra
I WANT	desire & regeneration	Scorpio
I SEE	philosophical insight	Sagittarius
I USE	discipline	Capricorn
I KNOW	intuition	Aquarius
I BELIEVE	compassion	Pisces

The Signs of the Zodiac also have rulership over the various parts of the body.

Sign	Body Part	Connection to Spirit, Mind & Emotion
Aries	Head	mind-spirit
Taurus	Throat & Neck (thyroid)	desire center
Gemini	Arms & Lungs	conscious mind
Cancer	Breast & Stomach	motherhood, nourishment & home
Leo	Heart	capacity to love
Virgo	Small Intestines	where assimilation occurs
Libra	Kidneys	balancers of the body
Scorpio	Sexual Organs	reproduction-regeneration
Sagittarius	Hips & Thighs	philosophy-movement
Capricorn	Knees	structure -humility
Aquarius	Ankles	freedom - intuition
Pisces	Feet & Lymph	compassion - understanding

Consider the magnificence of the human body !

THE SIGNIFICANCE OF TWELVE FOR THE HUMAN RACE

Can you see that the influence of the twelve signs of the Zodiac and the HUGE part they play in the interpretation of your natal chart?

There are twelve signs of the Zodiac.
There are twelve houses of the Birth Chart.
There are twelve planets, although to date only 10 have been discovered.
There were twelve tribes of Israel.
There were twelve apostles with The Christ.

TWELVE is the number signifiying Collective Consciousness!

What does that mean to you?

Have we been working toward this goal for centuries?

Could this have been paving the way for the New Age of Understanding?

Collective Consciousness – the Universal Awareness of creating a greater world.

Collective Consciousness – the Oneness and glory of ALL Creation.

Collective Consciousness – the Brotherhood and Sisterhood of ALL Mankind.

Collective Consciousness – the beginning of the promised fulfillment of this long awaited Aquarian Age!

ARE YOU READY?

CHAPTER FOUR

THE PLANETS

THE PERSONAL PLANETS

SUN
MOON
MERCURY
VENUS
MARS
JUPITER
SATURN

THE COSMIC PLANETS

URANUS
NEPTUNE
PLUTO

The Personal Planets:

Sun
The Real You – that Inner Spark of Divinity

Moon
The Gateway to the Soul – Emotions and Memories

Mercury
The Mind – in Daily Conscious Awareness

Venus
The Sharing of Love and Beauty

Mars
The intense Energy drive

Jupiter
The Philanthropist and Philosopher

Saturn
The Teacher and Disciplinarian

The Cosmic Planets:

Uranus The Universal Knowing

Neptune The Mystical Connection

Pluto The Miracle of Rebirth

The Influence of the Planets

The planets of our universe are **massive** centers of vibration that are the basis of astrological knowledge. Actually, you could call it "star chemistry"– the blending of vibrations sent forth to earth from these huge planets in our universe. It is the astrologer's task to examine these planetary cycles (as seen from your birth chart) in order to understand their relationship to you. This is the key to help you unlock your vision and understanding!

It is then that your path of destiny and the fulfillment of your life plan becomes an open book and a reality check!

The astrologer will draw your birth chart using your time, date and the longitude and latitude of your birthplace. Suddenly, as you see the process of the Planetary Cycles explained, you begin to understand the blending and weaving of your energies as they swirl into your life pattern. However, it is only **when** an astute astrologer relates this life pattern to your current and past experiences – that the magic of your understanding BEGINS!

It is very important to understand the influence of the planets, and their planetary positions as they relate to you at the time of your birth.

They are the most prominent points to remember as they are the "heart" of your natal chart – the significance of your birth.

There are ten planets the astrologer considers: Sun, Moon, Mercury, Venus, Mars, Jupiter, Saturn, Uranus, Neptune and Pluto.

It is this comprehensive knowledge of planetary influences that will enable you to better understand how and why you act and react as you do.

Indeed, there is a plan to your life and to every life born.

The joy and happiness you meet in life are but the beginnings of contact with an infinitely greater harmony within yourself!

The sorrows and afflictions you face in life are the important factors that will shape and change you!

Indeed, it is while you are under the confining and limiting influences of your difficult planetary aspects that you will long for the freedom of thought and action.

As a deeper understanding of your astrological map seeps into your consciousness, your energies will begin to free themselves to express the important purpose for which you reincarnated.

It is then you will work with the fullness of your energies, until you become **one** with them and your great destiny plan!

Indeed, the charts of the greatest people are often the most sorely afflicted! Yet, it was only when they exercised a determined will and believed in the greater good that they could create the success of achievement!

So it is with each one of you! It is only when you understand the heart of each of your difficulties, that you will discover what adjustments need to be made. Remember, great souls are often faced with the hardest circumstances until they learn how to direct their innate power to achieve the success they desire.

Yes, the planetary vibrations DO describe how your energy flows.

HOW you USE those energies is up to you!

THE PERSONAL PLANETS

The ten planets moving in this universe, have always extended their blessed energies to assist you in developing your own awareness of life, physically as well as spiritually.

However, they are divided into two sections: The Personal Planets and Cosmic Planets.

There are seven personal planets that will deal directly with your individual life.

These Seven Planets have been in our Solar System since the beginning of time. It is these seven planetary vibrations that will be studied in order to assist you in understanding your personal journey in life. These powerful planetary energies will help you gain insight into yourself and your relationships with others. These energies are here to enable you to develop, grow and prosper in wisdom, grace and enlightenment.

Keywords for these magnificent seven planets – (known as the Personal Planets)

Sun Vital Life Force

Moon Emotion /Soul Memories

Mercury Reason /Communication

Venus Love / Beauty

Mars	Dynamic / Energy
Jupiter	Philanthropy / Inner Vision
Saturn	Structure / Obstruction

Let us continue our journey into discovery of our real selves!

THE SUN
Giver of Your Life Force

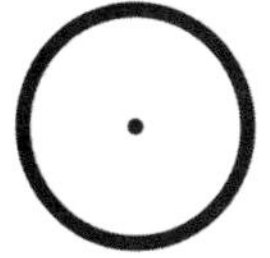

The I AM – the spiritual essence of man
"I Am that I Am"

Astrologically, the Sun is the most powerful influence of all. Your entire universe revolves around the Sun. Just as the external Sun is the center of your physical universe, so is your SUN placement in your chart the center of your own personal universe.

The physical SUN sustains all life on this planet. You cannot survive without its life-giving rays. Everything revolves around the Sun on a physical level. The primal energy from the Sun not only fills you with life, but also transmits energy to every planet in the universe. It is a fiery energy defined as masculine and energetic. Note the different power of the Sun's rays each month as it travels through the yearly calendar. The energy of these rays also heal as they move through the twelve signs in different ways.

This powerful SUN energy assists the minerals, hidden deep within the earth, to come forth – the minerals that hold the secrets of time.

This powerful SUN energy assists the plants to grow abundantly – plants that nourish as well as heal.

This powerful SUN energy assists the animals, considered by some to be our lesser brothers and sisters, to grow and evolve in their own way.

Finally, this powerful SUN energy assists you, the human being – in the ability to reason, to communicate and to share this sacred primal energy that constantly surrounds you.

On the inner spiritual level, the Sun is the symbol that signifies the eternal spirit – the unfolding of spiritual consciousness – the love that flowers from the human heart. It leads the soul to understand its immortality – that the spirit of man is temporarily clothed in mortal flesh.

The sign the Sun is in at the time of your birth is the pathway in which your spiritual nature will evolve this time around. It is the single most important factor in the interpretation of your chart. It will describe your basic energy force – your WILL – and how it influences your consciousness.

Since the Sun represents your true "inner self" (the real you, the spiritual essence of you), the astrological sign of the Sun, at the time of your birth, will color and define exactly how the sun's energies radiate through you. This is your Sun-Sign.

The SUN is your center post and the guiding "light" of your life force!

Remember the beauty of the glorious rising Sun – its brilliance seeming to extend beyond the horizon.

Feel the shine of that great Sun as morning awakens to sweet birdsong heard in the distance.

> Bless that enormous beauty of the brilliant Orb as it lifts up a new day – pouring forth steady rays of courage to the human heart.
>
> Sense the shimmering dew kissed by its golden rays – showering its unending love to our universe and beyond.

THEN apply those wonders to your own personal Sun – your own awakening of your Spirit within – your own Sunrise showering good will. Feel the joy at being created in such a wondrous world!

This is the beginning of the true meaning of your Sun placement in your chart.

Ponder upon this mystery of your life force – how it rises within you – and how YOU will shine! In essence, the SUN is the CENTER of your very being! It's quality, element and placement in your chart will be vitally important to you!

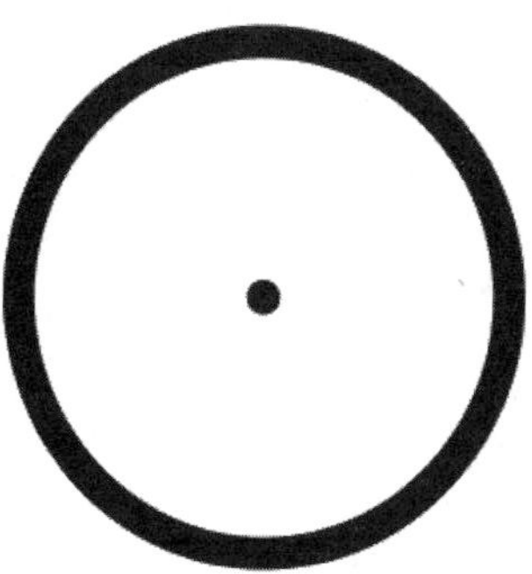

This dot represents the golden seed of the spirit within you – It is your link to the Eternal Source!

THE MOON

Soul Consciousness – Emotions & Feelings

The Gatherer

"The soul knows what the mind cannot imagine and the heart cannot forget." St. Claire

Astrologically, the Moon is a reflection of the Sun's rays mirrored back to us in the darkness of night. As the earth turns away from the life-giving energies of the Sun, the Moon will shine, luminously and with gentler rays, illuminating the darkness with tenderness. Therefore, the moon becomes, in astrological terms, the sphere of the soul. It symbolizes the eternal soul memories of humanity. The Moon is interpreted as the sensitive reflector of your moods, your emotional feelings, and your soul memories!

Why is the moon so mysterious?

Astrologically, the moon has a great significance for each individual. The astrologer will interpret the placement of the moon at birth as the emotional and instinctive awareness of each individual as well as his or her capacity to absorb and react to situations. I have always suspected that when we entered this earth plane at birth, we came through the moon and brought with us a soul portion (understanding) of our past lives to guide and remind us of what we needed to do! Indeed, your moon placement will help you to understand the unique way you express yourself emotionally, with your various moods and subconscious memories.

The moon mirrors all the natural instincts you bring into this life. It describes the mother you would attract, the home life you need, the environmental influences that would best shape your emotional attitudes. When you view yourself from this angle, that changeable, restless part of you becomes more decipherable. Your home and early life will take on more meaning.

The moon absorbs and reflects the psychic nature of the individual. As the moon rules all the tides of water across the full surface of the earth – on the inner level, the moon symbolizes the human tides of emotional situations and the yearning for calmness and inner peace.

The moon has held mystery and wonder for many civilizations. Most nights, the moon, waxing or waning in its various stages, became a constant companion. It has been a guide for all people of the earth since the beginning of time. Even though it has been poetically referred to as a "burnt out corpse", each night it sits like a patient parent reflecting the solar rays of the great Sun to a sleepy world. Simple herdsmen considered the moon a faithful friend on lonely nights. Ancient farmers used it as a dependable guide for fruitful plantings and harvesting.

Today, thanks to the onslaught of scientific research, the imaginative lore surrounding this luminary has been replaced with a better understanding of the electromagnetic impulses transmitted through it. The moon, flashes off the energy of the Sun in the form of an altered ray. Sensitive instruments have also shown that the lunar influence is quite real. The phases of the moon bring modulations in the earth's electric and magnetic fields. Neurological and psychiatric cycles parallel seasonal and lunar changes. "Effects" of the moon seem more pronounced on unstable individuals. It is not suggested that the moon affects human behavior directly, but electromagnetic force of the phases of the moon do seem to affect different people at different times in different ways. Astrologically, the moon holds great significance for each individual. Its placement in its astrological sign, at birth, will describe your emotional and instinctive awareness quite accurately.

The moon has great significance on human behavior. The aboriginal races had their religious ceremonies, as well as agricultural and political activities, regulated by the four phases of the moon – the new moon, the waxing moon, the full moon and the waning moon. The ancient Magi determined religious festivals by the moon's phases and gave advice accordingly. Even today, dates for various religious observances are still determined by the position of the moon, including the Christian holy day of Easter.

The Significance Of The Full Moon

The full moon has always intrigued people, not only for the majestic beauty of its brilliance, dominating the evening sky, but because of the noticeable and odd behavior of certain people at that time. The full moon period seems to affect people "emotionally" as well as physically. Even songwriters, tuning into romance, have immortalized this feeling in their music.

There has been interesting research done on the full moon, indicating some people's enzymes and hormones seem to be more stimulated at that time. Heart rates may go up and some people are more excited. Notice I say some, not everyone! Check the police blotters and see the increase of crime at this time. Check the emergency wards and medical records and observe the flurry of unusual activity with accidents and bleeding problems. Some individuals with anti-social behavior and psychotic tendencies seem to go wild at certain full moons.

Astrologers know these effects are caused by the interaction of the moon's pull with the earth's gravitational and electromagnetic fields. A person's susceptibility lies in how that particular full moon placement in the heavens correlates to their own astrological chart.

If the gigantic oceans and large bodies of water all over the earth are controlled by the magnetic pull of the moon's vibration, then would it not be logical to watch your own reactions and analyze the influence of certain full moons in your own lives? Remember, all human beings are made of 70% water. Watch the full moon periods as they come and go. See what astrological sign the full moon is in on the particular month you feel "something". See how it applies to the aspects in your natal chart.

How does your emotional nature and home life appear to you? Check your moon placement.

THE MOON

See the moon high in the heavens – a shining beacon to all who search.

See the moon high in the heavens – a changeable orb giving stability to every night.

See the moon high in the heavens – sharing a muted glow of concern to a sleepy world.

See the moon high in the heavens – guiding – comforting – a faithful companion to those whose tears fall in nightly sadness or loneliness.

See the moon high in the heavens – and know all is as it should be, with its stillness and its meditating rays of introspection.

The Moon reflects the light from the Sun.

The symbol is the half moon. Here the moon symbol indicates your emotional feelings and the heightened sensitivity of your human nature. It is your reflective inner soul of past memories which become stronger as your intuition develops and your awareness of life unfolds.

MERCURY

The Gift of Mind
The Communicator

Since it is so close to the Sun, Mercury has been called "The Messenger of the Gods". It is the planet of reason, mind and intellect. This mercurial vibration enables the human beings to think and to communicate with each other in every way – in every moment. The minerals, the plants and the animals cannot communicate with the fluency and wondrous ability that allows the human being to do so.

The planetary vibrations of Mercury rules over anything related to transmitting thoughts and ideas. It influences messengers, postmen, advertising, printing, clerks, typists, secretaries, salesmen and those engaged in literary pursuits. It is a natural vibration for the air signs because of its swift and agile ability to think and speak. Mercury enhances the conscious mind in the sign of Gemini.

Mercury is the educator as well as the communicator. This intellectual vibration uses its mind as its avenue of expression. It uses the hand to write, the tongue to educate, and the mind to reason. This influence is vital to your every day life. The mercurial faculty of the mind is masculine and of the air element – using the brain, with all its mental facilities, as its avenue of expression.

The nervous system, is also intimately connected to the mind and the brain. There is the belief (through the metaphysical side of astrology), that most nervous afflictions are not due to disease but to wrong or misplaced thoughts. Thus, hostile attitudes and negative thinking could further lead to the poor functioning of the senses and the emotions. Have you ever heard of psychosomatic problems?

Mercury rules the 3rd house of the chart which is the House of communication (Gemini House). Mercury also rules the 6th house of the chart which is involved in health (Virgo house).

Both are deeply involved in thinking and analyzing, comparing and scrutinizing. This heavy duty use of the mind can affect health if not properly understood.

How do you see Mercury helping you in your chart placement? Hopefully, you are now aware of the vital need for these qualities of communication and education? Without the abilities of the Mercury vibration, it would be very difficult to live on this earth plane.

Mercury – with winged feet and winged helmet – swiftly swirls thought vibrations, person to person.

Mercury – the power station lying between the great SUN and the Earth – a wondrous connection of planetary radio broadcasting.

Mercury – the miraculous expression of the human race – using tongue and hand – breath and thought

Be grateful for every breath you speak with – every gesture you motion with – every step you walk with! This is the great gift of Mercury!

The symbol for Mercury is the Sun, the moon and the cross.

The Moon symbolizes the vast respository of emotion and memory crowning the great Sun. The Sun symbolizes the great spiritual life force within each person. Together, they are connected to the Cross which represents our workplace – the earth plane. These connected symbols all lead to the fulfillment of the communicating human being.

Mercury, being so close to the Sun, represents a sort of mediating power station from Source of Life to the earth plane.

VENUS

Priceless gift of LOVE
Love and Beauty

Venus, being so close to the earth, appears as the most luminous of planets. It is the planetary vibrations of Venus that manifests the principle of love on earth, of attraction, of joy, gifts and benefits. It calls forth the deep, spiritual emotion called love and has the ability to attract others. There is a gentleness and grace that surrounds this influence, bringing a beauty that is not seen in other planetary vibrations. Its magnetic charm directly affects the higher side of human nature.

Venus is the LOVE planet. The heart is its vantage ground. There is the young love of youth. Then there is the developing of unselfish parental love. Finally, and hopefully realized – the greater spiritual love – "To love thy neighbor as thyself". This is the flowering of wisdom that comes with age and experience. Living in this objective world, we quickly realize the need to find the true meaning of love. The Venus energy injures no one. This planetary vibration is the most healing of all vibrations. It is the true vibration of love, unselfishness and charity!

Venus is also the mother of the Fine Arts, showering a deep appreciation for all the finer, elevated gifts that man can envision, be it music, art or any other higher expression of refinement and beauty. It can transmute the reproductive instinct into the deepest emotion of love in all its beauty. This is the vibration of harmony and beauty that fills the art houses, the museums and the opera houses with the beauty of the artist and composer. Indeed, Venus signifies harmony, sweetness, gentleness, refinement and, at its best, cooperation.

A footnote: The Venus vibration has a subtle, receptive power that attracts and absorbs the Mars energy. Together they transmute this energy into human love – conjugal, maternal, and paternal.

Can you describe your love nature by the placement of Venus in your natal chart?

VENUS - the sweetness of the inner self – allow true love to flow through you!

VENUS - the giving of the outer self – allow true love to find you!

The Venus vibration and its influence –

The Venus vibration is the connection between cooperation and joy!

The Venus vibration is the fulfillment of beauty and harmony!

The Venus vibration is the bearer of grace and refinement!

The Venus vibration gives the shining energy that makes living a gracious statement!

What are some of the things the Venus vibration can indicate?

The illuminating colors of the artist – awakening the canvas.

The arc of a hand carved frame – haunting in its craftsmanship.

The pealing chimes of children's laughter – innocence aloft.

The gentle breezes of universal love – caressing the trees.

The full bud of spring – promising the lushness of summer.

The vibrant splash of autumn – preparing the deep slumber of winter's journey.

Every moment in every way, Venus has its own beauty, where love reigns supreme!

The symbol for Venus is the circle with the cross.

The circle is the glorious Sun aspect of the higher self. The cross is the symbol for the earth.

The Sun connecting to the Earth is our reality plane. Here Venus is the combination of the higher aspect of our spiritual nature.

Venus is the vibration of Love we need to cherish in order to flourish!

MARS

Dynamic Energy
The Warrior

The planet Mars brings the message to each of us of the insistent need to create, energize and lead! This planet gives off a red color indicative of its fiery character. To accomplish much and to avoid misuse of personal energy – this is the great challenge of the Martian vibration.

Mars is a positive, masculine energy that rules the head (Aries) and the reproductive organs (Scorpio). Mars also rules iron and iron is a necessary element in the blood. Without it, the body becomes unfit to do anything. Mars also indicates inventions, ceaseless activity and a consistently high energy level, physical as well as sexual. A strong Mars vibration in your chart can either assist you to develop the noblest of virtues – courage, strength of character, self confidence – or, through anger and self assertiveness, you can use its energies to be very destructive. Mythology called Mars, the God of War.

Mars, ruling Aries, is the sign of a born leader, a fearless warrior and a true pioneer – all capable of using dynamic energy or reckless force. This planet also rules Scorpio, indicating the sign of great passion hidden amidst the depths of emotion. Here, the dynamic energy is more inward and cautiously silent. The Scorpio energy contains a powerful ability to generate healing for others.

If we did not have the Mars vibration, we would not be able to cope with this world. Possessing a strong constitution, the Mars vibration will propel great independence as well as a positive and self-reliant attitude. We need its strength and belief in self, especially when things get difficult or hard to manage. This energy enables us to cope with climatic changes and to replenish physical energy, which is of necessary importance in the drive to conquer matter.

During the Middle Ages, the kings were given the symbol of Mars as the "orb of power" at their coronations. This symbol denoted kingly power and they used this symbol to challenge the world with that power.

Where is the Mars vibration in your chart? How do you use your strength and power? Do you have the ability and courage to fight for what is right and fair and good, or do you believe "might makes right"? Do you use your strength and power for your own embellishment, or do you consider the greater good of mankind? How will you use this great power that continually energizes you?

Mars - the vibration of power, force and courage.

Mars - vibrant energy, red glowing – fearsome to behold.

Mars - the call to arms – when courage is needed.

Mars - vibrant leadership – instilling courage and belief in self.

Mars - the power, the drive – the hardy optimism of life.

Mars - our lifeline to self reliance and the courageous heart.

How this vibration will fight will depend upon how your Sun energy is used.

The Mars vibration indicates one of two directions:

1. Be courageous and fight for others.

or

2. Use energy unwisely by rushing into action without forethought.

The choice is yours!

The symbol for Mars is the circle with the arrow slanted upward.

The circle represents the solar energy of the Sun with the arrow pointing up – the arrow represents the fighter – the warrior.

Understand how your Martian energy flows from you.

Be prepared to use it wisely! It is a great gift!

JUPITER

♃

Philanthropy & Benevolence
The Philosopher

The vibration of the planet Jupiter allows benevolence to flow – and with it, the kindness, the compassion, and the greatness that exemplifies the best of mankind. It is in this awareness that individuals strive to help one another. This philanthropic, cheerful, optimistic, honorable vibration is the mark of the humanitarian personified.

The generosity of spirit and the kindness of human nature are the trademarks of this great planetary vibration. Good fortune is usually signified by its placement and aspects in your chart. Emotions, under this great planetary vibration, are usually honest and beautiful. The Moon and Venus may express emotion and tenderness but the Jupiter vibration expresses benevolence, and generosity. It extends great vision as one always seems to see and understand the big picture. It expresses nobility in its finest form.

On the other hand, in its lesser vibration, it can mean excess and self indulgency. Jupiter rules Sagittarius and is the largest planet in the universe. It has nine moons. This planet's vibrations are usually distinguished from other planetary vibrations by the way it likes to do things – the "big" way.

Sagittarius is a fire sign with its own set of qualities – very different from the other fire signs of Aries or Leo. This is a fire sign of expansion – expansion of emotion – expansion of thought – expansion of action as well as the opportunity for great soul growth. Many fine athletes and champions have a strong Jupiter placement in their chart.

Everything is big here. This vibration of Jupiter (the ruler of Sagittarius and co-ruler of Pisces), always seeks the cause and the base of action. It inquires into motives and purpose. We can call it the planet of the judge and the lawmaker. Under its influencing rays, the moral qualities of man begin to develop. Nothing is petty or small. This great Jupiter energy stands for soul growth, expansion and magnanimity. Therefore, when you radiate benevolence, you do become a dynamic center through which many blessings flow. "As you sow, so shall you reap" is always a constant reminder of what our thoughts and actions can create.

The sign and placement of Jupiter in your natal chart not only indicates how you have used these energies in past lives, but also the possibilities of greater future development in this current life. Your opportunities are here! This is the life, now, where the possibility of further developing your compassion, your vison, your philanthropy are clearly in your hands, your mind and your intentions. This Jupiter vibration within you will help you to expand and further blossom into the magnanimous human being you really can be!

Where, in your natal chart is the Planetary vibration of Jupiter? Where do you radiate benevolence and wisdom for mankind?

JUPITER

Jupiter – The archetype of greatness.
The understanding of all that is good and whole.
The merciful "milk of human kindness".
The steady builder of truth and justice.

Jupiter – The majestic vibration of optimism.
The flowing magnanimity of purpose.
The uplifting emotions of understanding and encouragement.
The benevolent caretaker of whose vision widens hope and uplifts the weak.

Ella Wheeler Wilcox put it succinctly when she wrote the following:

"…the deathless me of Me…
Is part of that eternal source called God
He who knows and knowing never once forgets
The pedigree divine of his soul
Can conquer, shape and govern destiny,
And use vast space as 'twere a board for chess
With stars for pawns;
Can change his horoscope to suit his will;
Turn failure into success...
And from preordained sorrow harvest joy"

The symbol for Jupiter is the moon and the cross.

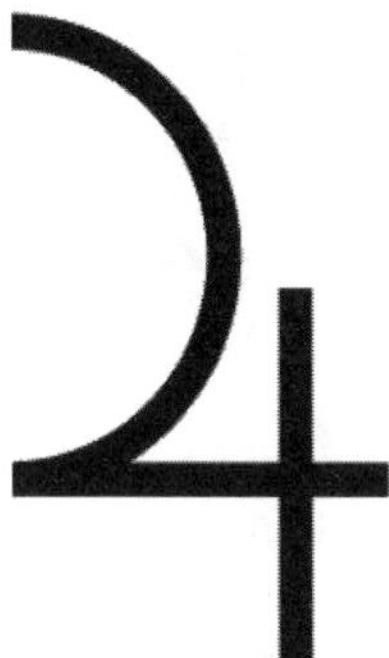

The moon refers to the subconscious soul and its potential inner growth. The cross depicts the earth plane upon which we can grow, develop and prosper.

SATURN

♄

Structure and Obstruction
Our Greatest Teacher Vibration

Saturn is a gigantic planet with nine moons and a series of concentric rings. Its vibration is most powerful in a different and very real way. Saturn rules Capricorn and is co-ruler of Aquarius. It is our greatest "teacher" vibration.

The lessons you learn in life are indicated by your Saturn placement and aspects. It stimulates your conscience – pulling at the core of what you have been and helping you to create what can be. There may be obstacles you will need to face in order to overcome – difficulties you may need to solve in order to bring closure to the past. Indeed, past memories – karmic awareness and the understanding that "what you sow, so shall you reap" is a reality!

With Saturn, you are faced with obstacles to overcome.

With Saturn, comes the opportunity to do the necessary hard work.

With Saturn, comes the lessons to gain the self discipline (essential in achieving and overcoming any difficulty).

With Saturn, situations appear that are so necessary for spiritual growth.

Please remember, you are never given what you cannot handle! A closer examination of your chart will reveal how you can overcome and conquer whatever weakness, difficulty or affliction you may face. Your potential for greatness and success is described so vividly in your astrological map – the picture of the heavens when you were born.

There is also balance here. Your chart will signify what worthy qualities you have brought with you to assist in facing, changing and conquering whatever karmic problems you need to repair, whether they be within you or relating to other people. (Karmic means situations brought back from past lives, and never resolved in those particular lifetimes).

You will find, when it comes to sensitive points in your chart, you WILL feel the Saturnian vibration strongly. Watch your planetary patterns and the situations that arise with it.

They are laying out the blueprint for you to clearly understand. This will be the time to **face** reality, and your own forgiveness! Everyone makes errors, be it in this life or past ones.

The gaps and holes you now find in your life – the sadness and frustration that nag at you – are all part of the rebuilding that must go on in order to achieve a wholeness again – regardless of what department of life is affected.

These Saturn cycles (seven year cycles) come and go with a definite plan. The great lessons of these Saturn cycles will rest on the condition of your foundation. Saturn is the ultimate builder, therefore:

a. If you build on a poor foundation,
b. If brutal honesty with yourself, as well as others, is not total,
c. If the desire to do the "right"thing, or create the "right"atmosphere is not genuine or real,
d. If you cannot be ready to really forgive whomever, or whatever has transpired in the past, THEN all will collapse and you will continue the crazy merry-go-round! Why? Because your foundation of thinking and loving and feeling has holes in it! The Saturn aspects are explaining to you your need to build a clear, honest foundation to your life.

Many astrologers approach the Saturnian influence, when applied to its planetary cycle as "bad" – or an "evil influence". NOT TRUE! It is your interpretation that concludes it as "bad". Actually these obstructive influences will be blessings in disguise! Check the placement of the Sun and Saturn and see what struggle the ego will encounter during this particular time. Saturn is like the parent forced to discipline a wayward child. Your Saturn cycle, pertinent to you, is the time you must stop, think, and be careful as you **analyze** the situations in your life and your actions as well as reactions!

Saturn is the cosmic timekeeper. Many times, as we face with this cycle, it brings forth what we have created somewhere along the long line of our lives. When the time is ready for us to achieve and overcome, this Saturn cycle comes along and clarifies it. Sometimes the harshness of necessity forces us to see the need for a better, more noble way to deal with difficult or obstructive situations than our lower nature could be prone to.

This heavenly timekeeper Saturn, keeps endless records. When the time is ripe for new experiences, your ego is born and Saturn's placement and aspects will indicate what you may need to work out. The position and sign of Saturn may indicate certain inharmonious vibrations which your ego has infused into the all pervading ethers. Everything is recorded on the Akashic records. Edgar Cayce, the great sleeping prophet of the 20th century, stated clearly in one of his deep trances – "everything in your life is recorded, down to every jot and tittle". (meaning every period and comma) NOTHING escapes the thought forms we generate – whether kind or mean spirited – optimistic or pessimistic – happy or hopeless.

Once you gain understanding through the difficult dimness of misunderstanding or the pain of obstruction, then watch how quickly your difficulty or obstruction smooths out. Watch how you will finally realize the glorious awareness of your path and purpose!

Remember, mental anguish, pain and suffering are the inevitable consequences of the indulgence of the senses. Examine your Saturn cycles! Be very aware of what situations you may need to pay attention to. Then watch the miracle of how you can grow into the greatness that is your birthright!

Those whose Saturn aspects are favorable from birth, can instinctively help you to understand how to live a frugal, chaste and moral life. Their conscience will be highly developed, having taken many lifetimes to achieve. They are sometimes called "old souls". These hardy individuals are a great example of the steady Saturn vibration.

To repeat, your placement of Saturn in your natal chart cautions that unless you build your house (your life) with a secure foundation (with your thoughts, words and deeds) and with meticulous care – then you will have a fall!

This is the fact and the reality of the Saturn teacher vibration. It is not to be feared or disliked! If this teaching vibration seems to be severe and even unfair to you in this lifetime, then – Stop – Look – and Listen to your inner self – your conscience. If you can develop some understanding of a situation and its purpose, then be grateful that your very understanding and openness can reduce, and even obliterate the past. It can be achieved with open heart and patient awareness!

Where is your discipline and structure in your chart?
What are the weaknesses and learning lessons you need to understand?

THE GREAT PLANET- SATURN

Saturn - the insistent reminder of "What you sow, so shall you reap".

Saturn - the strict taskmaster whose guiding discipline is sorely needed.

Saturn - the stern, relentless teacher – payback time if not behaving.

Saturn - the builder of righteous living and clear conscience.

Saturn - the holder of the inscrutable wisdom of the ages.

Saturn - the memories & lessons of the darkness of pain & frustration.

Saturn - the memories and lessons in the light of understanding & wisdom.

An Explanation:

To those readers who feel my assessment of Saturn may be too harsh or heartless, please understand its necessity. The Saturn cycle is NOT a gentle vibration. It is the strict and demanding Teacher in every sense of the word. Its vibrations are stern, practical and just. It is the ultimate of the great axiom, "Do unto others as you would have them do unto you!"

Saturn is the last of the seven personal planets. It is a formidable planet whose planetary vibrations can guide you to understand what you need to do in order to balance out – to behave – to forgive – to understand!

If it seems unfair to you, then again – Stop – Look – and Listen! There is something important going on that needs to be remedied. If you can open your awareness and be able to understand any difficult situation or relationship a little bit, then you have already begun to pave the way to reduce (and eventually obliterate) any past action or deed that needs balance and justice.

"Saturn (is) that condition in the earth's solar system to which all insufficient matter is cast for remolding, as it were." Edgar Cayce from reading 945-1.

"Insufficient matter" means things left undone – "remolding" is being reborn in the righteous (right) way of living! Indeed, the steady character training and self-discipline is what releases the limitations of the Saturn vibration. This is the great, noble task of Saturn.

The Saturn symbol is composed of the same cross and crescent moon as seen in the planet Jupiter. Only this time, the cross is on top indicating the power of the material world.

♄

It is in this world we live where conditions, relationships or any other difficulties are grappled with. As the moon's rays stimulate past emotions and memories, it is the Saturn vibration (the material world) where your conditions and relationships are worked out. Only through your understanding and sincere effort can YOU RELEASE YOUR OWN LIMITATIONS!!

Build your foundation well!

THE COSMIC PLANETS

There are THREE COSMIC Planets: URANUS – NEPTUNE – PLUTO

These cosmic planets were discovered in the last 153 years! Imagine, for thousands of years, these cosmic planets were not even dreamt of, let alone discovered. Then suddenly, from 1781 to 1933, these three planets have been discovered.

Uranus was discovered in early 1781 by William Herschel.
Neptune was discovered by Galle of Berlin in 1846.
Pluto was discovered in 1933 (near the ending of the Piscean Age).

The planet Uranus - the higher vibration of the planet Venus - universal love.
The planet Neptune - the higher vibration of the planet Mercury - other Dimensions.
The planet Pluto - the higher vibration of the planet Mars - transmutation.
Everyone is now ready to grow into these elevated superconscious cosmic vibrations!

These cosmic planets are very special! These three planets, because of their longer cycles, affect billions of people, all at once, throughout the world. These cosmic planets are raising the vibrations of Venus, Mercury and Mars to a higher degree as the energies of the earth are speeded up.

Elevated consciousness is growing throughout the earth plane and many are becoming very receptive to these higher vibrations. (In this sacred study of astrology, it is indicated that there are two more planets, of higher vibrations, to be discovered when they become finally visible to earth). I believe they will be the higher vibration of Jupiter AND Saturn.

In the last 2000 years, the Piscean Age has come and gone. It was the Age of Pacifism and the Golden Rule as taught by the great Master of Christianity. We learned that we did not die, but simply moved from one dimension to another. HE laid the basis for the coming Age of Aquarius!

NOW is the time for the Aquarian Age –
NOW is the time for a deep and vibrant spiritual awakening
NOW is the time for the most thorough cleansing of negativity from the earth –
NOW is the time for universal love to finally create a universe of brotherhood & peace!

URANUS

Beginnings of the Aquarian Age
The Equality of Each Human Being

Uranus was discovered in 1781 and has four satellites. It is considered the higher vibration of Venus – where human love transcends to become truly altruistic – knowing no bounds – no creeds – no limitations!

The real meaning of Love has been misunderstood for **too long**. The Mars passion (desire) rather than the Venus love (giving) has been generally mislabeled as love. That is on the physical plane solely. But, on the spiritual plane, the Uranus vibration stimulates a love that surpasses all. It produces the true humanitarian who loves everyone equally – for who and what they are, and where they are in time, space and growth. This is called universal love!

This great, freeing, erratic, unconventional cosmic planetary vibration of Uranus appeared around the time of our great American revolution. The very air of independence was everywhere! This period gave rise to the true belief that each and every human being is created equal!

Now, two hundred years later, we have to come further to realize that inequality comes **only** from each person's own lack of self-love. They still need to be tested by certain trials and lessons to really overcome. Uranus, with lightening speed, will breakup and disintegrate what is not right in your life. Ponder on this!

People, who are strongly influenced by Uranus, are lovers of freedom, rebellious at the least restraint, independent, intuitive and inventive. They possess an extreme nature. Depending upon the placement of Uranus, some individuals can be erratic, quick tempered and somewhat unconventional. The vibrations of Uranus are always sudden, and unexpected. Situations develop out of the blue, either with ease or difficulty, depending upon the quality of your intention.

When you have a prominent Uranus in your life plan, you would be well advised to not act rashly. In the twinkling of an eye, this lightening vibration can produce a whirlwind in your life, tossing everything upside down. Change is the keynote. The old has to be destroyed before the new can begin! The Uranus vibration rules astrology. A strong Uranus placement in your natal chart will assist you in mastering this sacred science since you will have brought with you the strong gift of intuition as well as an innate understanding of Aquarian vibration.

Year 2004 – Uranus began its freedom journey through the sign of Pisces. You will start to witness a world-wide freeing from superstition – a deeper swing toward compassion and the REAL understanding of what freedom means. The consciousness of mankind will rise and with it, a greater understanding of the organized religions of the past 2000 years.

The influence of this planetary vibration will assist us to become freer – to become the shining beings we were designed to be – helpers – healers – peacemakers – earth workers and lucid teachers. We have all entered the Aquarian Age, where the entire earth and all that lives on it, be it mineral, vegetable, animal or human, will feel the higher vibrations of Uranus. Here mankind will have a magnificent opportunity to materialize the dreams of the past Piscean Age with all its new, stimulating and independent freedoms and inventions of this current Aquarian Age.

Indeed, inventions will abound – humanitarian efforts will increase – the awareness of self, in relationship to others, as well as to the Divine, will grow. The search for a connection to our higher self will dominate. The final awakening of the entire planet will glow in understanding as we all rise to the challenge of the gauntlet Uranus has thrown down to us. The new Age of Aquarius has begun!

Uranus - with a lightening strike, intuition unfolds truth.

Uranus - with genuine altruism – the brotherhood of man begins.

Uranus - with a crashing of false premises – the swift ending of false dogmas.

Uranus - electric – erratic – your efforts tumble if the direction is wrong!

Uranus - balance your spiritual nature with its magnificent abilities.

The Uranus symbol is composed of half moons, the cross and the Sun end.

The first half moon represents human nature. The second half moon represents the divine nature. They are joined together by the cross of matter, leading to the ultimate foundation of the Sun's power.

The Uranus vibration exemplifies how your human nature (half moon) can work with your spiritual nature (other half moon) on this physical plane of the earth (cross).

The final result is the unfolding of the dynamic life force of the SUN, within each of you, to create the inventions, promote progressive ideas and shower forth the intuitive guidance for the future course of the world.

NEPTUNE

Investigating our spiritual nature
Gift of Prophesy

Neptune was discovered in 1846. Its distance from our SUN is over three trillion miles away but its influence is very real.

As the first cosmic planet Uranus, works chiefly upon the higher vibration of human love lifting the human consciousness to a higher level, so does the second cosmic planet Neptune, work chiefly upon higher vibrations of spiritual energy that soars through the endless creativity of the sensitive, the mystic and the dreamer.

This mysterious Neptunian vibration gives rise to poetry, bestows prophecy and gives a deeper understanding of the delicate power of flowers and fragrance to the human race. (Have you ever heard of the Bach Flower remedies?) Did you know sensory gifts can also elevate thought? Neptune is the higher vibration of Mercury where thought merges with feeling into a higher inspirational, spiritual level.

You are now working in a totally different realm – a realm of the finest of human thought. It has been stated that the vibrations of Neptune do not belong in business. However, very successful businessmen have that uncanny knack of "knowing" what to do and with perfect timing. These are hunches directly from the Neptunian vibration.

Neptune, like Venus rules music. In generations gone by, the value of inspiration and song was taught through rhymes and singsong – comforting in time of need. Music, the universal solvent indeed possesses the ability to "soothe even the savage beast".

As Uranus, the higher vibration of Venus, lifts the **love** nature of the human being out of the personal level to the higher humanitarian level – then Neptune, the higher vibration of Mercury, lifts the mind and vibrates the intellect to a universal understanding. The physical body actually becomes more sensitive to everything around it. Many fine psychics and mediums develop such a sensitized physical body.

We are now talking about your dormant spiritual abilities! Everyone has them. Everyone has a Neptunian vibration in their chart. You will find, with a strong Neptunian influence, the artistic taste will be heightened to a greater appreciation for the beauty of form, color and sound. However, unless one is very grounded in reality, these visions and ideas may lack practicality. Remember, Mercury is the planet that vibrates the light of the intellect from the physical SUN. Since Neptune is the higher vibration of Mercury, these visions and ideas are more on the artistic, inspired mode of the intellectual effort.

On the other hand, if the Neptunian placement in your chart has difficulties with other vibrations, then your attitude and intention is very important. Individuals with a strong Neptunian influence are easily swayed by their emotions. They are very, very sensitive. Because of these psychic tendencies, you can touch the inner planes of the spirit world very easily. You need to avoid anything that clouds the senses, especially drugs and alcohol. Since you are a trusting and giving individual, your "feelings" can guide you in most of what you do. However, you must be on guard against deception, treachery or fraud. Be patient with yourself. The rewards will be great.

Note well: Since each person's life is the outcome of some former living, you now have a valuable opportunity for soul growth. NOW is the time to rise above any such difficult circumstances and change! Forgive yourself and go on for you are your own finest healer!

Your fantastic Neptunian abilities carry the inspirational and futuristic hopes for mankind. Develop and apply them well. The world waits patiently for your gentle love – your giving nature – and your healing spirituality. We so need your energies and inspiration!

Where is your Neptune planet in your chart? How do you radiate creativity and sensitivity?

Neptune - The vibration of the ultimate mystic – the seeker of the divine within everything.

Neptune - The psychic – the clairvoyant – the healer.

Neptune - This world is NOT your prison. Hurry up and let the sunlight shine in!

Neptune - The poet – the composer – the artist – the literary ability to inspire.

Neptune - Your destiny awaits you – the earth and all its inhabitants wait!

The symbolism of Neptune is the trident, the symbol of power over the oceans.

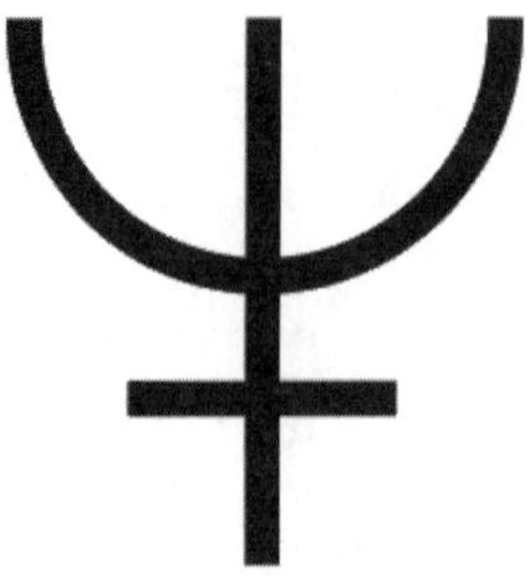

Indeed, water has always signified emotion.

The moon shape of Neptune is a cup that gathers and holds emotion – the basis for each person's soul memories and experiences. This cup is supported by the cross (matter) indicating that the potential for great spirituality must be grounded in the Earth in order to support a true inspirational life.

PLUTO

The deep cleanser- The true inner healing of the soul

Transformation

This mysterious planet Pluto, was discovered in 1933 and is the farthest in distance from our earth. It has an unusual cycle, eliptical in movement. It is the planet with the most unusual vibration.

"From dust thou art and to dust thou shalt return" brings to the forefront the tremendous power of Pluto and its influence over life and rebirth. It has a great magic about it. We use the Phoenix bird symbolism for Pluto. It is the image of a Phoenix bird being consumed by fire, only to rise again from the ashes, reborn! Healing – regeneration – transmutation – the highest form of insight into the underlying forces of life – all are stimulated by the vibrations of a planet just discovered only 73 years ago and at the farthest point from earth.

When the Pluto energies move as indicated in your astrological chart (your picture of the heavens at the time of your birth), you will feel these deep changes, moving you from the caterpillar stage into the most beautiful butterfly. These radical changes produce a transformation within your life. Pluto sets the stage, when action, or inaction, or certain activities (going on, subconsciously, for a long time) suddenly become a basis for consideration. You will suddenly wake up to situations that seem to finger a turning point in your life. Actually, you may think that, but the truth is these seeds of change were deep within you all along, until the correct timing came forth for you to go through a thorough change!!

It is hard to believe a creeping caterpillar, with its limited motion, can actually turn into a creature of delicate beauty and fly! So it is with human nature. This seemingly radical change will take place in your awareness – your very being – your understanding when the time is ripe for it to begin. It starts with all the little events of your life that have gone unnoticed, until that culmination of a turning point appears! How you will change!

Pluto is, indeed, the grand master of the deep cleanse. It may not come easily as some of these transformations can come like a volcanic eruption, taking you by surprise. All along, the molten lava was churning and changing you from deep inside. At other times, it can come like a tidal wave of overwhelming proportion. However it comes; the magic works. The transmutation is real and you are a far better, far greater, more awakened human being.

Bless the Plutonic vibration!

On a worldly scale, this Plutonian energy paves the way for the beginnings of the new world (already dawning) – the Age of Aquarius! With Pluto in the sign of Sagittarius, religions, laws and philosophies, will undergo a real and deep cleanse. There will be profound changes. The spiritual consciousness will become increasingly more active as the vibratory energy of Pluto increases on earth. The very consciousness of human beings will rise significantly. The many and varied countries across the earth, regardless of race, or language or creed, will become more aware of the need to live constructive lives.

They will feel the Plutonic vibration of cleansing and regeneration as it slowly spreads across the many lands, despite the selfishness and greed that now exists. It will be contagious as the "awakening of a higher consciousness" begins to mushroom.

We are on the cutting edge as this new Age begins. The birth pangs of any birth – the tumult and chaos of any change – may seem unending, but changes are coming. Removing and upsetting your former ways of thinking and acting do not come easily. The transformations and changes the Plutonic vibration brings, will stimulate your lives and the lives of many around the world in quiet and mysterious ways. It will encourage a change of consciousness and the desire to live a more peaceful life. What greater gifts can be desired at this time in history than these?

Where is this changing and mysterious vibration in your chart?

Pluto - The majestic gathering of little events along the path of life.

Pluto - Sudden, the mind sees clearly – awaking the subconscious to its destiny.

Pluto - Deep change takes place – one existence ends – another begins.

Pluto - End of the caterpillar – beginning of the butterfly.

Pluto - Casting off the old – transforming to new.

Since Pluto is so newly discovered, we are still finding out many things about its powerful and intense vibration. The Pluto placement in your chart is most important. It will symbolize the deep and transforming changes that will suddenly appear in your life and consciousness.

However, although these changes seem to appear suddenly, it actually has been a deep, underground current that was working all along in secret and intense ways. When you finally become aware of certain happenings, it will be the Plutonic vibration that brings it forth – to change – to transmute – to heal deeply to the depths of your very soul.

The symbol for Pluto is the Sun caressed within the Moon and supported by the cross of matter – the Earth.

Here Pluto symbolizes our path in Life. At the bottom, is the support of the many experiences of life (on Earth) moving upward through the illumination of the reflected Light of the moon (soul memories) to the awareness and fulfillment of your inner spirit (the great SUN).

NEVER FORGET:

You are creating your own world and fulfilling your own destiny, with a great boost from these magnificent cosmic planets!

Uranus
Neptune
Pluto

They all cast their long orbits around the world with meticulous care – surrounding us with the quickening awareness:

for the greater good for ALL,
for the highest aspiration from ALL,
for the deepest spiritual love for ALL!

These are the blessings from our great Cosmic Planets!

CHAPTER FIVE

THE HOUSES

The Twelve Houses of the Astrological Chart

(The Departments of Your Life)

THE TWELVE HOUSES of the ASTROLOGICAL CHART

Houses and Signs are Different in Meaning

Each HOUSE describes a division or section of your life.

Each astrological SIGN will be seen to color the house whose cusp it is on.

THE DEPARTMENTS OF YOUR LIFE

First House	Your Rising sign, Personality Traits & Early Childhood
Second House	Your Earning Capacity
Third House	Your Environment & Communication
Fourth House	Your Home and your Foundation
Fifth House	Your Children and your Creativity
Sixth House	Your Work & Health
Seventh House	Your Partners
Eighth House	Your Matters of Death and Regeneration
Ninth House	Your Philosophy & Religion
Tenth House	Your Discipline & Career
Eleventh House	Your Friends & Group Work
Twelfth House	Your Seclusion and Rebirth –the Karmic connection

The ASTROLOGICAL SIGNS have a very strong influence in describing your approach or behavior (as you have seen in the chapter on SIGNS). In these HOUSES (the departments of your life), there is a relationship between the signs of the Zodiac and the House placements, as you will see below:

THE FIRST HOUSE

The symbolic ruler of the first house is Aries.

The first House begins at the place of sunrise – 6 A.M. Even though you may have a different Rising sign on that first cusp at birth (due to your birth time), there will always be a touch of the Aries influence in this House. It is the First House and begins with the first astrological sign – Aries. It is the point of 6 A.M.

The First House explains your Rising Sign, Personality Traits & Early Childhood.

This first house is assigned to all beginnings, including the childhood years, as well as the physical appearance and certain characteristic movements. This first house is most important since it expresses your self-awareness and how you responded to your early life experiences. It will indicate the tendency of your disposition, as well as the conditioning of your young environment. All these factors must be considered when analyzing the first house. Your impressionable nature, your developing personality, and your early developing of habit patterns are established and described in this House placement. I often think this first house lays the ground work for the rest of your life.

This is the I AM House

THE SECOND HOUSE

The symbolic ruler of the second house is Taurus.

Even though there may be a different Rising sign on that second cusp (due to your birth time), there will always be a touch of the Taurus influence in this House. The Second House begins with the second sign of the Zodiac – Taurus.

The second house is assigned to all earning power and tangible assets. The Taurus influence is concerned with living in the material world and possessing the comforts and pleasures that are deemed, by them, to be necessary in this life. You can look upon it as the house that deals with personal property, personal worth and personal success.

This is the I HAVE House

THE THIRD HOUSE

The symbolic ruler of the third house is Gemini.

Even though there may be a different Rising sign on that third cusp (due to your birth time), there will always be a touch of the Gemini influence in this House. The Third House begins with the third sign of the zodiac – Gemini.

The third house is the mental area dealing with your environment, your everyday travel and your ability to communicate. The Gemini influence is concerned with all matter of communication: speaking, writing, travel and even thought patterns. It links people through thought and experience. Relationships with siblings, neighbors, and anyone else they are in contact with, takes center stage. The conscious mind needs to exercise caution as well as discrimination in whatever it is thinking.

This is the I THINK House

THE FOURTH HOUSE

The symbolic ruler of the fourth house is Cancer.

Even though you may have a different Rising sign on that fourth cusp (due to your birth time), there will always be a touch of the Cancer influence in this House. The Fourth House begins with the fourth sign of the Zodiac – Cancer. It is the point of Midnight.

This fourth house rules the home, your foundation, your mother and your spiritual base. Here is indicated your home base and its conditions, your spiritual growth, and your type of mother. It relates to your sense of security. It also represents endings and old age as well as soul memories from the past. This area of parental conditioning is very important. Remember, this is a moon ruled House. Emotion rules the day!

This is the I FEEL House.

THE FIFTH HOUSE

The symbolic ruler of the fifth house is Leo.

Even though you may have a different sign on the cusp (due to your birth time), there will always be a touch of the Leo influence in this House. The Fifth House begins with the fifth sign of the Zodiac – Leo.

The fifth house rules the heart, and indicates your children, whether they are of the flesh or are products of your creative imagination. It indicates great creativity, your self-expression and the performing arts as well as places of amusements – even the gambling instinct. It symbolizes creativity at its highest and empowerment through love, whether it is physical, emotional or spiritual. This is the energy and determination of the Leo fire!

This is the I WILL House.

THE SIXTH HOUSE

The symbolic ruler of the sixth house is Virgo.

Even though you may have a different sign on the cusp, there will always be a touch of the Virgo influence in this House. The Sixth House begins with the sixth sign of the Zodiac – Virgo.

The sixth house indicates your health and the type of work you radiate to in your life. There is a strong desire to be useful and productive. The Virgo influence does NOT like the limelight. They prefer to work behind the scenes. Diligent in the performance of their tasks, they are very health conscious and will use their mental as well as physical abilities in the most constructive and practical way.

This is the I ANALYZE House.

IMPORTANT! SUMMATION OF THE FIRST SIX HOUSES:

This is Your PERSONAL area of life.

The first 6 Houses of the Zodiac indicate the influence of your PERSONAL Action and Reaction to Life around you and within you.

These Houses deal with how YOU react, cope and function with others, on a personal level – attitude, earning power, communication, home, self-expression, as well as work and health.

The first Six Houses also deal with the lower half of the chart. This is the area of your personal life, attitudes and reactions. These houses are hidden from the world and are considered personal. These are the Houses dealing with the personal side of your life.

INDICATION FOR THE LAST SIX HOUSES:

Your Dealing With Other People

The last 6 houses of the Zodiac will indicate their influences on how an individual deals with OTHER people!

These are reactive house placements, showing how we react, adapt, and function in the outer world of human relationships. The last Six Houses deal with the upper (top half) of the chart. This is the area of the outer world where everything is seen.

THE SEVENTH HOUSE

The symbolic ruler of the seventh house is Libra.

Even though you may have a different sign on the seventh cusp (due to your birth time), there will always be a touch of the Libra influence in this House. The seventh House begins with the seventh sign of the Zodiac – Libra. It is the point of sunset.

The seventh house indicates your partners – the types of people you will attract, and your close relationship with others, one on one. It describes the marriage partner, the friends you will attract, all types of counselors, or anyone involved with contracts, legal affairs or public contacts. It deals with individuals on a one-to-one basis.

This is the WE ARE House.

The distinction: WE ARE (7th house) as opposed to the I AM (the 1st house).

The EIGHTH HOUSE

The symbolic ruler of the eight house is Scorpio.

Even though you may have a different sign on the cusp of the eighth cusp (due to your birth time) there will always be a touch of the Scorpio influence in this House. The Eighth House begins with the eighth sign of the Zodiac – Scorpio.

The eighth house rules sex, death and regeneration. The Scorpio influence deals with inherited money, or property, insurances and taxes as a result of death. It is the house of your partner's money. It also deals with the mysteries of subtle energy forces of the human body, the healing energies and occult knowledge. The ability to contact other planes of existence beyond the five senses also exists – the higher levels of wisdom and healing ability.

This is the WE HAVE House.

The distinction: WE HAVE (8th house) as opposed to the I HAVE (2nd house).

THE NINTH HOUSE

The symbolic ruler of the ninth house is Sagittarius.

Even though you may have a different sign on that ninth cusp (due to your birth time), there will always be a touch of the Sagittarius influence in this House. The Ninth House begins with the ninth sign of the Zodiac – Sagittarius.

The ninth house deals with the philosophies and religions of man. It also deals with anything that travels over 24 hours and any long distance travel. It deals with the great bodies of law, religion, and philosophy as well as teaching in the institutions of higher learning. Finally, there is the continual development of spiritual and philosophical thought through book writing, teaching and publishing. The influence here is great wisdom, inspiration and insight to uplift mankind through the development of universal consciousness.

This is the WE THINK House.

The distinction: WE THINK (9th house) as opposed to I THINK (3rd house).

THE TENTH HOUSE

The symbolic ruler of the tenth house is Capricorn.

Even though you may have a different sign on that tenth house cusp (due to your birth time), there will always be a touch of the Capricorn influence in this House. The tenth House begins with the tenth sign of the Zodiac – Capricorn.

The tenth house deals with your standing in the public eye, your reputation, your career. Your actions are there for all the world to see. Whatever you do, nothing is hidden whether you are famous or infamous. For your reputation, honor or dishonor will be an open book. This house will indicate strong ambition and the drive. Self discipline, hard work and patience are the key traits. This house demands great care and conscience. The tenth House begins at noon.

This is the WE USE House.

The distinction: WE USE (10th house) as opposed to I USE (2nd house).

THE ELEVENTH HOUSE

The symbolic ruler of the eleventh house is Aquarius.

Even though you may have a different sign on that eleventh cusp (due to your birth time), there will always be a touch of Aquarius influence in this House. The Eleventh House begins with the eleventh sign of the Zodiac – Aquarius.

Your eleventh house rules dealing with groups and creative group work. This will be demonstrated by working for and supporting associations that communicate the need for universal love and caring. The humanitarian ideal runs strong! Friends are also very important to them and are looked upon as "family". This area indicates strong intuition and an overwhelming love for humanity.

This is the WE LOVE House.

The distinction: WE LOVE (11th house) as opposed to I LOVE (5th house).

THE TWELFTH HOUSE

The symbolic ruler the twelfth house is Pisces.

Even though you may have a different sign on that cusp (due to your birth time), there will always be a touch of Pisces influence in this House. The twelfth House begins with the twelfth sign of the Zodiac – Pisces.

This house rules the hidden situations in life; unfinished business, isolation, seclusion or retreat. It rules the accumulation of subconscious memories, attitudes and experiences. There is a strong possibility of emotional blocks that can cause one to try to escape reality. This house placement reveals the area of life in which the individual can most deceive him or herself, and the areas of life where he or she gives the most of him or herself. It rules the memories of past deeds and misdeeds (karmic). It is only by consciously facing and correcting the restrictions of their life, that they will go beyond their limitations and draw upon the deeper levels of inspiration. Only then will they be able to discriminate between the subconscious impulses that are constructive or those that are not.

On the other side, there is great wisdom and depth of understanding here. This house placement indicates kind, loving and sympathetic souls. Their empathy towards the less fortunate is superior to all vibrations and born out of the highest expression of human love. They possess the ability to be great channels of mystical inspiration. This house favors artistic creativity and places of solitude where they can work out their karmic problems.

This is the WE UNDERSTAND house.

The distinction: WE UNDERSTAND (12th house) as opposed to the I ANALYZE (6th house).

When you divide the chart in half (top half and bottom half), there is a further way of interpreting the chart.

The first 6 houses (1-6) deal with your PERSONAL attitudes (intimate)

1st House	Self-awareness
2nd House	Material resources
3rd House	Practical thinking
4th House	Home base
5th House	Creative self-expression
6th House	Work, health and service

The last 6 houses deal with your attitudes of RELATING with others (broad)

7th House	Relationships
8th House	Death issues & Regeneration
9th House	Vision and Philosophy
10th House	Career
11th House	Humanitarianism
12th House	Compassion

Now, go find your birth time and place, and have your birth chart drawn up by a reliable astrologer or a good astrological computer program. You will be using Siderial Time as well as date, time and place.

You will find different signs on each cusp and the ten planets in different houses and under different signs. After understanding the meaning of the planets, the astrologer will study, with studious respect, the placements of the signs, the houses and the planets – all synchronized and blended with conscientious effort.

This is where your great mystery of life begins to unfold!

This sacred science of the signs, planets and houses will show you how the electro-magnetic vibrations interact within you and your environment every moment of life. Awake or asleep, you are constantly feeling these subtle vibrations (and their cycles) stimulating your body, mind and very being to think, act and feel. However, in grasping the understanding of the planetary cycles and aspects that appear in your natal stamp (chart), please remember the future is always in the state of becoming! Never forget – Free Will is the KEY – the magic ingredient here! Once you have a clear awareness of your strengths and weaknesses, just know your understanding and determination, can change or redirect ANYTHING!

Transmutation is the healing path to a full and productive life.

Note: Due to the specific calculations of your own natal time and place, the signs on each House WILL change. The calculated astrological chart is a picture – a photograph of the heavens, at the very time of your birth. Each of you will have a unique and different chart, just as each of you have a unique and different path to travel in your lifetime!

THE TEACHING CHART

(Note: This is NOT a natal chart. This chart is for teaching purposes only).

All the astrological signs, from Aries to Pisces, have a symbolic relationship to the houses. On the Teaching Chart you will see these signs as the symbolic ruler of each house.

The Teaching Chart

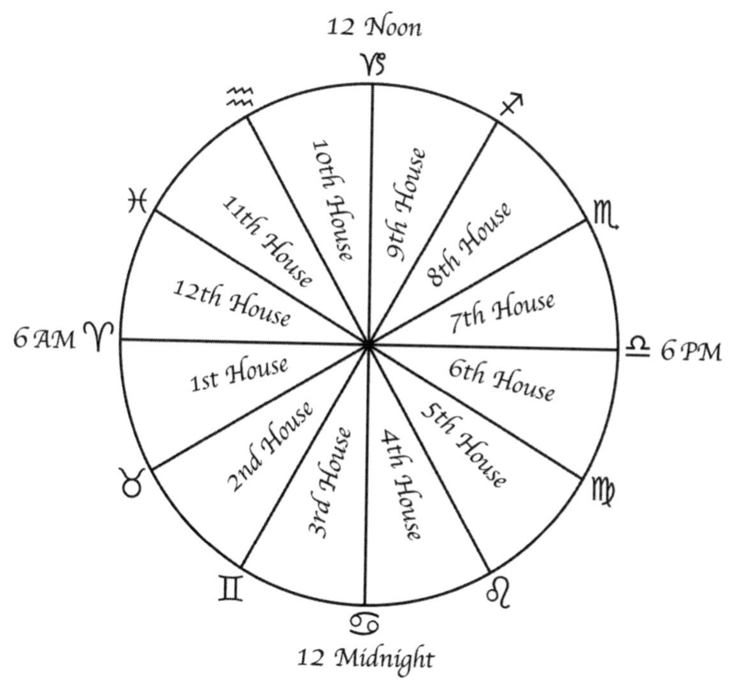

Is There Such A Thing as a BAD CHART?

This poses an interesting question. I find a certain mentality of thought that seems to pervade these times. It is one where you feel you are the "victim" – the helpless individual – the one born to "gloom and doom" – where you want to place all your inadequacies of any situation on a quirk of fate. Fate has no quirks! Your life is a combination of circumstances, inherited tendencies and personal attitude all revolving within a cyclic sequence of planetary timing within your natal chart!

Actually, this idea may frighten some of you, if you are unaccustomed to taking care of yourself in life. This is especially true if you are dependent upon others to give you the direction that is rightfully your birthright within the perimeter of your intelligence. Never thinking for your self, or lacking confidence to do so, can allow other people's thoughts and opinions to influence and control you. You are told what to do, what to wear, when to move, etc. This is astounding, yet so easy to understand, as we are all programmed from childhood to take direction until we reach some mysterious, undefined stage called "maturity".

Unfortunately, some of us never relinquish that childhood dependence. Others may feel, with great intensity, that they must have been born under an unlucky "star". Perhaps, this could explain why they are so unhappy or so unfortunate. The Truth is NO ONE is born to have an unhappy life!

You may be born to face unhappy lessons – but NOT an unhappy life!

That is your choice!

The ultimate culprit is the lack of a constructive outlook or not taking positive action rather than blaming the inharmonious placement of planets at birth. Perhaps you need to pay attention to your inharmonious energies. They are inharmonious for a purpose! Could this lack of harmony be one of the greatest lessons you need to realize and learn from? Is it possible that these inharmonious vibrations are here to wake you up in order to learn how to master them? Remember, no birth time is ever casually allotted – you helped create your natal chart.

It is difficult to go along with individuals who feel they are "trapped" in life. Although it may be real in the physical world, what is really trapped is their attitude and outlook! A glass of water is half full or half empty. It all depends on HOW you see it!

Some people do seem to have a life of luxury and ease. There is a reason for this and a good chart analysis could explain it. It has to do with how they handle harmony within themselves. However, this does not mean they have a perfect life, except, perhaps, from your point of view. If you were placed in those very shoes, maybe it would not seem so ideal to you, with your own set of abilities and needs this time around.

Inner growth and the appreciation of life are the "gutsy" things that last. Money, position, social popularity are all ephemeral. Like gossamer wings, they decay rapidly with whim and the fluctuating economic tide. Investigate your "own" value system before you "envy" the other person and his seemingly "fortunate" life. Believe it or not, each of you have exactly what you needed when you entered this world.

How you use your talents and personal brilliance now becomes your responsibility! Each of you have been born with a distinctive planetary pattern, when, if properly understood, can be a valuable, sensible map of personal perception. You are not doomed in life! Fatalism has no place in true astrological interpretation!

Astrology is an effective tool to discern your highs and lows. The planetary cycles will constantly swing through your circumstances to stimulate your behavioral tendencies, but it is you who acts it out! The current suggestions, in daily horoscope columns rob you of the ability to understand yourself. If you follow them, they will fog your vision and dilute your common sense. Curiosity is one thing, but enlightenment is another! Read "good" material on the subject. Learn for yourself what makes you tick! Learn what your tendencies, inclinations, capabilities, weaknesses and strengths really are!

No Human Being is born with a Bad Chart! No one is ever destined to become a bad person. WE all have free will! If you believe the opposite, then your simplistic thinking belongs in the Prison of Ignorance. The truth is, you were born with a distinctive planetary setup, when, if properly understood, has a message of great importance. It can be your most important road map in guiding you along the bumpy highway of life!

Astrological interpretation is based on accumulated and organized knowledge dealing with the planets and their cycles. It deals with the electromagnetic influences you were stamped with as you entered this world with your first earthly cry. When you can begin to understand, even a little of the complexity of your own vibrational energies, think of how you will be better able to cope with periods of stress and tension, refusing to allow them to pollute your thinking and your very environment!

You will then understand that situations, easy or difficult, come in cycles, and they DO NOT last forever! It is only your approach and your reaction (spawned from ignorance or poor attitude) that seem to last – and last – and last. Your stressful cycle has moved on, but still you persist as it is forever! That becomes the time to check your chart and check your attitude!!

NO ONE IS DOOMED in LIFE! Damnation comes only if you allow such negative attitudes to prevail. The choice is yours! In understanding your planetary cycles, you will find they will mirror back the inner you – your circumstances – your environmental background – your path in life. With patience and the deep desire to understand, all will be revealed to you as your clarity of vision grows! If you feel you were born unlucky or born into an unfortunate situation, then you had better look within for the answer!

You are what you think and feel more vividly than you ever realized. Each of your actions bring with it the opportunity to grow. Each difficult situation presents the opportunity to conquer the unstable and weak tendencies to which you are prone. It is the lack of a constructive outlook and lack of a positive frame of mind that is the REAL problem!

Attitude makes the difference – be it a passing thought or gigantic event!

Attitude can turn gloom and difficulty into a festival of joy!

Attitude can take misfortune and lead you into a fine opportunity!

Open your eyes! Open your mind! Analyze, observe and begin to **comprehend** the POWER that lies within you.

Know that the Great Gauntlet of Freedom as been handed to you – your Free Will!

Use it with confidence and the wise gathering of your life experiences. Slowly, and surely you will finally begin to glimpse the enormous power that lies within you to accomplish whatever YOU WANT TO DO!

CHAPTER SIX

THE MAJOR ASPECTS

The Energy Patterns of Your Life

A. It is a Matter of Degree

Conjunction- Power points
Sextile - Opportunities
Trine - Rewards
Square - Obstacles & Challenges
Opposition vs. Co-operation

B. Is There a Possibility of Past Lives?

ASPECTS
The Energy Patterns of Your Life!

This sacred science of astrology is intimately linked to your first breath. It is this breath that stamped you with the vibrations of the planets and their aspects. What a momentous time it was for you as you entered this planet earth.

This pattern of your planetary placement was not accidental. It was a planned event you had chosen. In effect, your natal chart is a reflection of the strengths you came to work with and the weaknesses you will need to attend to – until you master them. Indeed, they are the reflection of the universe within YOU.

Do not be afraid of your weaknesses, or despise them. We all have them. There is NO perfect person alive. But the glorious realization comes when you can finally overcome them! How you will emerge a stronger and far better human being. How, in that overcoming and growing with understanding, you will grace the earth with such a healing vibration. Your energy will benefit all for the greater good – not just yourself. Every good and kind deed sends out such a note of harmony into this distressed world. And every note of harmony will eventually swell into a chorus of magnificent sound and beauty that will **hum** throughout your personal universe within your very being as well as the great physical universe that surrounds you.

It is the aspects of your planetary placements, and the planetary **cycles**, that will stimulate certain events in you life. It is the timing of these events which will be important to you! They are considered potentialities. These aspects will show planetary cycles in action. They will point the way to the development of your character and how you can either assist or hinder it. Free will is a strong component here. You will have a choice – to choose which way you want to go to determine your own growth throughout your present life.

Those who have not developed patience, conscience, and courage will bring into manifestation events which are the result of their own inharmony! Do you put yourself first – your will first – your desire first? Or, will your consciousness have risen to where cooperation and harmony become essential in dealing with situations and other people?

Selfishness is usually the keynote of ALL obstacles and difficulties. Therefore, difficult situations, if met with a constructive attitude and strong patience, can greatly mitigate any situation or difficulty.

There are five major aspects in astrology as well as subtle minor ones. In this chapter, we will deal with the major aspects.

Understanding these major aspects will be the most powerful KEY anyone can ever find in unlocking the difficulties, the doubts, the pain and the guilt in your life.

The Five major aspects are:

1. Conjunction
2. Sextile
3. Square
4. Trine
5. Opposition

POWER

1. The CONJUNCTON – This is a Power combination.

One major aspect of planetary vibrations is called the conjunction. It is indicative of much power and action as the blending of planetary energies combine with great force. This is where two or more planets conjoin within 8 degrees of each other. If the planets are conjoined with the Sun or Moon then 10 degrees are allowed. A conjunction is very dynamic and energizing! It usually indicates strong potential for personal expression and action. It is a POWER COMBINATION!

HARMONY

2. The SEXTILE - Opportunities Come Forth

The sextile is another major aspect of the planetary vibrations considered. This aspect energizes and paves the way for opportunity. Through utilizing this constructive, capable aspect with patient timing, a sextile will show you the way to opportunities and certain situations in life to capitalize on. With diligent work, you **can** succeed. This is indicative of opportunities arising for your benefit. A planet or planets within 60 degrees of each other planet (with an 8 degrees leeway) is in sextile. (It will be a 10 degree leeway for Sun and moon)

OPPORTUNITIES arise, and with them your abilities to accomplish your goals!

THE GREATEST HARMONY

3. TRINE - Rewards & Fulfillment

A trine is an aspect that brings much ease and fulfillment! It is what is generally called a gift you have earned from the past. Your abilities, in this aspect, will have an easy flow of energy in order to assist you in securing what you desire. You will find your good will and compassion will help you in securing the happiness and success you have earned from the good deeds of your past life (or lives). These qualities come easily to you (well earned) and this trine aspect is considered the most fortunate of aspects.

REWARD and FULFILLMENT come easily. Here the degrees between planets are 120 degrees (with an 8 degree leeway- 10 degree leeway for Sun and moon). It produces an abundant flow of energy.

DIFFICULTIES

4. SQUARE - Difficulties and lessons

The square aspect will describe the difficulties you will need to deal with as they come into your life. These are aspects where certain planetary vibrations clash inharmoniously.

A square represents disharmony – disharmony with one's self – disharmony with others – or both. These difficulties and limitations are areas you have come to balance out – to clean out. If you do not pay attention, these difficult habits and strong willed tendencies will become obstructions to your very own development and happiness.

The Planetary cycles (if in square aspects) will indicate the areas of your life that will require your personal attention and strong effort in order to change.

★You may have to adjust to difficult situations that will arise.

★You will need to continually strive for a better understanding of how to overcome your limitations in order to realize positive action.

As these squares signify difficult situations that come due with certain planetary timing, you can gauge preparation for these times once you are aware of them. These aspects, as they trigger the inharmonies that lie within you, will be the time to send out caution. It is the tolling of the warning bell to help you realize the necessity to use patience and understanding as well as the necessity to display discipline and structure. IF you really try, you WILL bring forth the true greatness of your being! Your difficult aspects will actually guide you to your own enlightenment!

Knowledge is power! Once you are aware, you can then understand how past misuse of your energies, thoughts or motives can now be redirected with a changing of attitude and an openness of heart. Nothing is ever fated! You are not destined to suffer! However, if you want to, then so be it. But, if your first desire is to truly become aware of your rash tendencies and headstrong ways, then you CAN change!

Sorrows and afflictions are merely factors used to shape and help you grow from within – to garner wisdom and understanding – to envision the larger picture of your life.

Just as iron needs to be bent to produce a form – just as stone needs to be chiseled to produce a work of art – so are you being bent and chiseled, shaped and formed, under the confining, limiting influences of your square aspects.

With determined and heroic effort, you **can** become the gifted soul you really are! When you finally understand this and work toward conquering the limitations you find yourself in – then, you will finally be freed to express your true self and fulfill your destiny plan! Some of the most profound turning points in life have started on a square!

Here the planets will be within 90 degrees of each other (with an 8 degree leeway – 10 degree leeway for Sun and moon)

CO-OPERATION or CONFLICT

5. OPPOSITION - this is the last major aspect where a planet or planets are within 180 degrees of each other (within 8 degree leeway – 10 degree leeway for Sun and moon) Here the aspects are completely opposite of each other.

This opposition aspect produces the opportunity to either cooperate or conflict. These vibratory planets of enormous energy are opposing each other. This indicates the struggle you have with another. There is a choice here! You can choose to work toward co-operation and conciliatory action or by opposing a situation or relationship, create disharmony, more difficulties and a willfulness that cannot be tolerated. Your free will is the key!! How will you handle it? The antidote for opposition is cooperation. Is that so difficult to learn – to give a little – to build a harmony together?

Pay attention to these oppositions! They will show you what you need to understand in order to overcome and bring forth the true greatness of your being. Indeed, these difficult aspects will guide you to your own enlightenment once you understand how your past misuse of your energies can now be redirected with a changing of attitude and energy.

You will need honesty within yourself to see the truth unfolding in these harsh cycles of squares and oppositions. You will need honesty with others as you deal with each situation that arises!

Now, you will read in many astrology books that the square and opposition aspects are evil or bad! This is NOT true! It may be considered evil by the person enduring whatever they have brought onto themselves. However, it is their lack of understanding or their lack of desire to curb their difficult tendencies that causes their frustrations to hinder them.

It may be very difficult to open yourself to reality when facing such problematic aspects as the Square and Opposition, but YOU CAN CHANGE! You can opt to use your free will and common sense to overcome any difficulty.

Remember, only YOU can start to overcome harsh traits, grudges, difficult relationships and misunderstandings. Only YOU have the power!

Therefore, please stop the anguish – open your eyes, your understanding, your heart and your common sense when you are facing a square situation. Allow change and GROWTH to come!! Remember a Square has a harsh angle that needs to be straightened out. It is a corner, like a right angle that STOPS the smooth flow of energy. Pause, analyze and look for ways to harmonize this difficult expression of your energy (the square aspect). Then, watch a miracle blossom for yourself!

As for the Opposition, dealing with others takes patience, consideration and a giving and taking. Remember, we are all the same underneath our miles of skin. Our emotions fall and soar with the same feelings. Our tears flow the same, whether in joy or pain. The greatest opportunity comes with an opposition. Here is where you learn to cooperate because an opposition is a whole that is separated into two halves. With cooperation, these two opposing halves become a WHOLE. It is no longer two opposites. but one completed whole, blended with harmony and peace, be it a marriage, a partnership, a friendship, an agreement or any other combination that brings opposing sides together.

Now is the time to use your free will with patience and understanding for yourself.

Your thoughts and actions are what counts! They do speak louder than words!

FORGIVENESS OF SELF

Once you develop this powerful awareness of your planetary vibrations (especially the inharmonious ones), you allow the path for true forgiveness to open up. Not only will this self-understanding help you to forgive others, but most importantly, it will finally bring to you the long needed **forgiveness for yourself!**

These difficult cycles not only offer the opportunities to be challenged, but the opportunities to be determined to overcome and transmute any difficulties in your past. Here is the opportunity to forgive others who may have harmed you Here is the opportunity to cleanse whatever heartache you may have caused – or heal any heartache caused by another.

We human beings were not meant to be so filled with guilt – EVER. If there is a transgression you feel responsible for – Okay! Then, try to work it out and grow from it. Get on with LIVING your LIFE! There is nothing so sad as seeing a guilt-ridden person. They beat themselves up pretty badly, always feeling such low self-esteem and unworthiness. So, what does guilt mean to you? Where does it come from and how can it be eliminated?

Guilt is the most devious form of self-torture – that sinking feeling of failure and fault that overwhelms you.

Guilt compares to that sink hole that swallows you up in the depths of agonizing self-doubt – where emotions are held captive by shame or self- blame!

Guilt – the whiplash of control that curls around you with insidious swiftness and tight command!

Guilt – the suffocating quicksand of feeling inadequate effort or emotional humiliation.

Guilt grinds your kind resolve into dust – when reason is lost and fear takes reign!

Guilt – the bottomless pit of despair – engulfing you in the dreadful pitfalls of confusion and disgrace!

Stop!

Why must this dark emotion force you to do things you do not want, but feel compelled to do?

Is it because your kind nature tries so hard to please?

Is it because of your feelings of inadequate effort?

Stop the unmerciful treatment by others that forces you into that tight corner of unbalanced compromise!

Stop the madness of what the human world has created – this monster within!

Guilt is a control mechanism created by mankind.

Whatever the situation – work it out – talk it out – but DO NOT HARBOR GUILT!

Action must come from LOVE not Guilt!

NOTHING is impossible to overcome!

Nothing can undermine you except your own self-defeating attitude!

Allow your will and intelligence to be exercised.

Remember, the FUTURE is always in the STATE of BECOMING!

Nothing is ever set as absolute if the "desire" to change and grow is really there.

I have found, in my experience as an astrologer, that what appears to be does not always have to be. Allow your free will and intelligence to guide your life. Utilize your common sense and the greatness within yourself to understand your inner emotional, mental and physical makeup. Allow the astrological information that describes you so well, to assist you! Allow your intuitive and psychic nature to evolve – your connection to greater Dimensions. Permit and encourage your endless pool of understanding to flow. Above all, dear souls, remember to treasure yourselves as unique and special as you really are!

★Let's see each morning as the dawning of a new day…a new start…a new chance to begin again!

★Perhaps then, we will all be able to really LIVE with greater self-awareness and self-realization.

★Perhaps then, we will all grasp the opportunity to repay any 'old' debts and misunderstandings and concentrate more on the ability to give service to others.

★Perhaps then, we will treat all living things, from the complex human being to the one cell amoeba, as a most precious and unique expression of love.

We are born to prosper, not to suffer!

Suffering is an elective in the school of life. It is not God–given! It was the mantra of the Piscean Age, now past. We have created our own confusion, our own grudges and our own fears ourselves. Use all your talents and abilities to get to the core of your suffering and end it! ONLY YOU CAN DO THAT!

You may meet others with whom you have had disagreements or somehow cannot even stand to look at. Perhaps you may even feel fear or loathing. Stop! Look at them with clear eyes and realize that is the PAST! This is the NOW! Reject negativity for it is a state of your own making!

THE KEY

By studying this great metaphysical science of astrology, you will gain a clearer perspective on life. You will assist yourself in freeing yourself from the clouded confusion of living. In astrology, the study of the signs, houses and planets with their aspects and cycles are the key to unlocking the mysteries and anguish of your life. They are the merciful key to living a greater life filled with a wider understanding yourself, and with the true appreciation of the quality of love.

Only your soul knows why you chose to be born on a certain day, time and place – and why you chose your parents, and those childhood situations in early life that would color the rest of your days. Deep within your quiet moments of reflection, your true self will surely begin to realize what you have come to accomplish. One day, it will all come together in a burst of understanding, as your intuitive nature will send that ray of enlightenment with swift knowing. Your questions will then be answered from the depths of your soul.

This is the Learning Plane! The fulfillment of your current life lies in your decision making power! It lies in how well you apply the wisdom of life's lessons.

★Now is the time to seek the deep understanding and awareness of your every action.

★Now is the time of opportunity to balance out any transgressions of the past.

This is the lifetime
    that can be built
        on the cornerstones
            of love, compassion and forgiveness!

★Now, this moment, this day, this time – TAKE the opportunity to learn, to understand, to grow and to prosper! Then watch how the beauty of your inner spirit will shine! I have found, as an astrologer, that what appears to be, does not always have to be! The future is always in the state of becoming!

There is a plan to each and every life!
Allow your free will and intelligence to fulfill it!

★Understand and utilize the knowledge of your soaring spiritual energies –

★Be grateful for the vastness of your sensitive, emotional being –

★Appreciate the magnificence of your brillant mental capacities –

★Protect your powerful INNER strength as a physical being!

Study your planetary patterns carefully and with wisdom.

Allow the astrological information (that describes you so perfectly) to help you to understand the BIG picture!

IS THERE A POSSIBILITY OF PAST LIVES?

That is an open, personal question that can only be answered by each individual. There have been many books written on this subject, but I believe it really comes down to your own personal feeling of inner knowing and acceptance, or outright rejection.

As an astrologer, I have met some people who do seem to remember a past life and can even trace how it has affected them in this life. I have also met others who reject this idea immediately – feeling this life is important – not vague memories of some undefined past.

Actually, does it really matter what we may feel or think? Isn't it what you DO in this life that really matters – this is the moment – this time to give the best of you to everything you do?

For those of you who have a strong interest in this area, there are some well documented events about life after death. There have been numerous situations where individuals, while on the operating table, stopped breathing and were pronounced clinically dead.

However, these patients, at that time of "death" were quite aware, at a deeper level, of moving into a bright light and meeting their deceased loved ones. While in this bright light, these individuals were cautioned it was not their time to leave the earth plane! They were told they needed to go back to their current life because they still had unfinished business to attend to. Suddenly, they began to breathe again and they DID come back to life! Do not these facts alone seem to verify that certain situations in their lives were still left unattended and needed to be settled – that the purpose and need for their life had not yet been fulfilled?

Dr. Elizabeth Kubler-Ross documented these instances in her books, calling them NDE (near death experiences). There seem to be many similarities with these experiences.

Dr. Brian L. Weiss, a noted psychiatrist, wrote enlightening books on this very subject when he discovered the existence of past lives, quite unexpectedly, through his practice.

Edgar Cayce, our twentieth century prophet, had reams of information on this very subject of past lives, received in his self–induced trance state. Could it be that all his efforts were to remind us of this long forgotten knowledge of the ages?

Just walk through any bookstore or library and you will find much documentation on this subject, especially on the memory of past lives through hypnosis and regression.

Of course, you may or may not agree with this line of thought, and that is understandable. However, perhaps this does mean these situations (repeatedly happening) are indicative of some greater Dimension of living of which many of us are not consciously aware. How does this approach affect the astrological interpretation of individual charts? Through my experience as an astrologer, it has been varied.

★Some clients have a past life recall that becomes important to understanding a very difficult situation they are facing and which is raised in their own astrological chart.

★To others, understanding past lives seems to unlock certain feelings and emotions that have hounded them and kept them from living productive lives until they could understand "**why**".

★To many more, who live in the moment, it does not mean much. To them, it is the NOW that is important!

★This is an individual, personal belief!

★The importance here is that your natal chart can show the way to remedy any difficulty that faces you now – in the present – if you can open your heart to love and your mind to see! It can point the way, but the effort and understanding is yours to accomplish!

During the time I was writing this book, Jody, a fine student and budding astrologer, asked me a question that puzzled her deeply. She had just finished reading a book on past lives and was coming to a conclusion that we come back to suffer and to face problems. "Is that what reincarnation is all about?" she asked, concerned and unsettled.

It is indeed unfortunate that this limited awareness of suffering happens to be a common view. The lessons we find in our lives need a far deeper understanding than such a fatalistic view that we come back to suffer!

We are all here to do good things, as best as our inner soul growth and understanding will encompass. Some may still fall into difficulties and willfulness. Perhaps, they need more time to seek understanding – to be made more aware of the fullness and abundance of life. Others yearn to see the big picture! It is at this point they will finally begin to develop a vision beyond this tiny, little world we have built!

Why should we envision a life of sadness, guilt and pain when there is so much joy and beauty in this world?

Do you really believe that the great Being of all Beings would create such beauty and love that continually surrounds us, and yet, on the other hand, force us to feel all the poor qualities of life as a punishment?

As you learn to see the big picture – as you learn to grow, and shine with love – you will be amazed at how you will understand your ever deeper spiritual connection. Remember the power of the SUN and its symbol. Never forget that dot within the circle, representing the SUN. It is that dot that represents the divine spark within you – the spiritual connection to the Creator of All Worlds.

YOU DO HAVE FREE WILL

★ It is ridiculous to think the stars, planets or any other influences control you!
★ It is ridiculous to think that past lives and past actions control you!

The study of your planets, signs and houses, with your aspects and cycles, are the KEY to unlocking the mysteries and anguish of your life. It can be a merciful key to living a greater life filled with understanding and fulfillment. There are valid explanations for the many things that seem so incomprehensible to you in this life. Allow yourself to see how you function and where your weaknesses and strengths lie. Only your higher self really knows "why" you chose to be born. When you finally understand the "why", and you will, then a great and wondrous gift will be unveiled: your purpose and path in this life!

★Now is the time to seek the deep understanding of your every action!

★Now is the time of opportunity to balance any imbalances of the past!

★The fulfillment of your life lies in your decision making power.

★The fulfillment of your life lies in how well you apply the wisdom of life's lessons.

★Deep within your quiet moments of reflection, your true self will realize what you have come to accomplish!

★This is the lifetime to build on the cornerstones of love, compassion and forgiveness.

FACING YOURSELF!

"As you sow, so shall you reap!" has always been our Learning Mantra!

Yes, there will be difficult situations that need your understanding as well as your willingness to give kindness and responsibility. It is the simple fact of facing yourself, within yourself. It focuses on the true understanding of the "eternal spirit" within and how your innate greatness can put back into balance any imbalance that may have been created. Once you realize this and try to do so, then you have conquered it forever. And in the process, enlarged your capacity to grow and flourish even more!

Then, there are gracious situations that shower forth the goodness of love and sharing. Do you realize how many kind and giving souls there are on earth who come willingly to teach – to assist – to help us mend our ways by simply showing understanding and patience – by showering generous love and kindness? These are the gentle teachers among us, usually in the most unsuspecting places. They live simple lives, doing what they can to encourage those among them to understand the goodness in life. I am sure you all can identify someone of this nature.

Astrology is part of the science of metaphysics, filled with wisdom and always dealing with the reality of your current life against the background of your total soul memories. The planetary chart, drawn from the time and place of your birth, illustrates what **you** have brought into this life – your talents, traits and genetic tendencies all translating into action to assist you in your current path in life. It is your special planetary arrangement that offers you the opportunity to grow and achieve as well as the opportunity to face and transmute certain situations that keep reappearing.

This is not awful! This is not to be feared! Here is the opportunity to grow both in wisdom and understanding as you face yourself. We ALL have lessons to learn and difficulties to solve. We all have great opportunities to share love and kindness.

THE FUTURE IS ALWAYS IN THE STATE OF BECOMING

The interpretation of any chart is always a challenging one. Please remember NOTHING is impossible to overcome. NOTHING can undermine you except your own self-defeating attitude. However difficult your aspects might appear to be, the future is always in the state of becoming!

The charts of some of the greatest people are often the most difficult. Yet, they were able to create extraordinary successes through their power of faith, inner will and clear vision. By penetrating the heart of each difficulty, as they did, you, too, can discover what adjustments are needed to be made and do so. Remember, great souls are often enclosed in the most difficult of circumstances until they learn how to direct their innate, God-given powers to do the specific work they came to do.

No difficult aspect, with its cyclical consequences, is ever set as absolute if the desire to change is really there. Nothing is impossible to overcome if the desire to grow is really there. When you try to mitigate a difficult trait, it is entirely possible, with your free will ability, to reduce its damaging effects, not only on your psyche, but also on those around you. With constant effort and awareness, it is entirely possible to redirect, reduce and even OBILTERATE the weakness or willfulness in your nature, and eliminate the damaging action or reaction that usually flows as a result of this weakness or willfulness. It is called transmutation!

I have found, in my experience as an astrologer, that what appears to be DOES NOT always have to be!

★Allow your free will and intelligence to guide your life!

★Utilize the knowledge of astrology to understand your inner emotional, mental and physical makeup.

★Allow your intuitive and psychic nature to evolve – your connection to greater Dimensions.

★Permit your endless pool of understanding and love to flow!

We are born to Prosper NOT to Suffer!

Suffering is an elective in the school of life! It is not God-given. We have created our own confusion, our own grudges, and our own fears ourselves. Use all your talents and abilities to get to the core of your suffering and END IT!

ONLY YOU CAN DO THAT!

We did not come to suffer! We came to balance! It is our thoughts and actions that cause suffering!

The abundance of life continually surrounds us!

Allow your life force and power of your thoughts to bring forth only Peace, Love and a gentle walk upon this Good Earth.

Treasure your temporary home with each lifetime!
Treasure, always, your spiritual connection to the great fountain of Universal Love !

CHAPTER SEVEN

What About "Your" Journey?

The Musings of an Astrologer

THE WHEEL OF LIFE

I am sure some of you patient readers are wondering what this last chapter (with its varied titles) has to do with the subject of Astrology. Well – it has everything to do with it! This metaphysical science has to deal with all the facets of life – all the parts of the human personality – all aspects of the complexities of living on this earth.

The Wheel of Life refers to the endless cycles of your charted course (your personal astrological chart). The planetary vibrations, in your particular pattern, will stimulate and flush open the parts of your soul that need attention and healing. Your greatest lessons and greatest achievement will be shown through your aspects and cycles.

Each time a delicate or painful part of your chart is touched through these cycles, (especially the Saturn cycle, since it represents a main factor in the path of your destiny), it is a time of learning – a time for you to reach out to your brothers and sisters – to your neighbors and co-workers. Evil cannot harm you for you have insulated yourself with your goodness!! Stretch out your love to even include those who wish to do you harm. Open your heart to understand their ignorance and fear and go on! It is not easy, but it is doable. And the more you do it, the more your understanding of the WHEEL of LIFE widens. The more you do it, the more you will grow in wisdom and inner peace!

There will be powerful periods in your life that will set the stage for when your actions or activities (working subconsciously, for a long time), will have a sudden realization of a turning point in your life. Once awakened, you will finally understand the meaning of living a more constructive life.

How we so need to understand the lessons we have come to learn. How we so need to cultivate and nurture our garden of life with clear vision and true forgiveness. Then, watch how abundance will flow into your world! And as we heal, the earth will heal!

Remember, you encompass all the qualities of the signs with the immense vibratory power of the planets in the various departments of your life as seen in the houses of the chart.

Astrology is a magnificent key to understanding your own personal path in this current life. Go find an astrologer who works in grace and light – or better yet, become your own astrologer and develop your own wisdom, awareness and grace!

WHAT MAKES A GOOD ASTROLOGER?

An astrologer is made of many things. First, astrology is **not** a cut and dried science where you can refer to any astrological author for the definition of let's say "Saturn in Cancer" or "Jupiter in Taurus", or any of the other myriad combinations astrologically available. There are many astrological authors on the bookshelves and many diverse opinions about the understanding and study of this science. However, this problem of describing certain aspects or planetary placements, or house areas, etc., can cause a beginning student to become confused. Some descriptions will be positive and others may be depressingly negative.

NOTHING is written in stone! This body of knowledge defies any set pattern of explanation. The young astrologer needs to develop his or her own intuitive abilities through the constant observation of the human drama surrounding them. Today, the mind's ability to tap into the cosmic energy is vast and unending. Be diligent, be sincere and your own abilities will flourish.

As far as cycles are concerned, this is the stability of the science. You must not expect a simplistic solution to let's say "Mars in Pisces" or "Venus in Aquarius" or any other combination. All the planets, signs and house placements are colored by the various aspects to each other. The total chart needs to be studied and correlated for real meaning.

Master the reading of the ephemerides (an astronomer's calendar used by navigators as well as astrologers). Understand the basic drawing of the chart with the planets in their corresponding houses, due to the time of birth. Examine the signs on the cusps of the houses, starting with the rising sign.

Spend much time observing and analyzing the planetary movements of your own chart and those around you. You will need time to analyze and become aware of the coincidences and/or discrepancies you may find. Everything is important, and personal experience is essential!

Be more independent and exercise your own thoughts, discoveries and opinions. The natal chart itself will be the positive proof you seek as you perceive various situations coinciding with the planetary cycles of the moment. In time, your own conclusions will become solid and you will find your way to becoming a true and astute astrologer.

Let me say it another way –

First – A searching and inquisitive mind is needed to delve deeply into the investigative work of examining your own actions, as well as other people's actions.

Second – **Observation and keen memory** serves well here. Life is a constant classroom and each human being will always be a special project!

Third – **Determination** to read, study and ponder the various points-of-view involved in this study. It is a most complex subject, entailing many factors. Eventually, you will become more independent and begin to exercise your **own** opinions, thoughts and discoveries.

Fourth – Patience is a most necessary ingredient as time answers many questions. Do not be so anxious to prophesize. ALLOW each individual to come to his or her own conclusions about their decisions or actions. What may appear to you, based on the chart reading, may be a limited interpretation based only on your "restricted vision" at that time. Allow the individual to come to his own conclusions.

Fifth – **Transmutation** is a very integral part of this sacred science of astrology. You, as a student of life, must know that anything can be transmuted, changed or redirected, however shocking or foreboding. Anything can be changed by the actual will and desire of the individual! If a cycle indicates a dire time, then help that person to realize his or her own capacity to overcome it, be it through patience, awareness or true honesty about themselves. Do not become an alarmist or a pessimist. Keep a steady flow of positive thought and energy moving. Allow the healing understanding that everyone is here to grow and develop into their own greatness. Destiny is in the making! The blueprint has been drawn, but it is not etched in stone. Remember, you are dealing with vibrant, living and breathing human beings. They must be made aware that anything can be changed, or redirected if there is the will to do so. They may be facing attitudes and habits that are long standing and may need serious repair as well as constant attention.

Sixth – **Compassion** is as necessary as the charts and cycles you deal with. We are all brothers and sisters under the skin. We all laugh and cry with the same facial structure! We all dance and ache with the same muscular tendons! We all breathe and love with the same beating heart! Know that many individuals will come to you because they want to see ahead and understand! If they wish you to tell them what to do – retreat! That is not true astrology! This great body of knowledge was meant to free each individual to make his or her own decisions. Guide each one to this conclusion, gently, but firmly. Then you can exult in the knowledge that your skill as an astrologer has helped you help anothers.

WHAT IS LOVE?

In this current generation, that are many types of love alluded to: steady love, emotional love, blinding love, fickle love, compassionate love, and tough love. The list goes on. But how can one isolate and identify an emotion that is so universal and healing all at once? Therefore I submit to you the following thoughts and feelings for your reflection and meditation.

Without LOVE, we are like empty drums with no sound.

Without LOVE we are merely lumps of clay with no soul – no divine spark !

Without LOVE, we are the silent destroyers of all that breathe.

Without LOVE, we have lost the pathway to the depth of emotion.

Without LOVE, we no longer exist on the higher plane of awareness.

Without LOVE, we are separated from the meaning of life itself!

So, let us realize what LOVE is –

LOVE – the elusive yet expansive emotion stretching from here to eternity!

LOVE – the comforting completeness of giving and sharing!

LOVE – that generous, enveloping flow of accepting and understanding!

LOVE – that true and best part of each of us – the Divine in action!

LOVE – the eternal touch of the finger of GOD ennobling our human nature – so vast, so expanding – it almost defies our understanding!

What greater glory –
What greater opportunity –
What greater gift is there but to LOVE!

WHERE IS YOUR WIZARD OF OZ?

The modern fable of the famous Wizard of Oz gives us pause to think about its deeper meaning. Dorothy (representing each of us) is thrown into never-never land by a vicious tornado. Lost in this strange land, she wants desperately to GO HOME again. She finds the Good Witch, who kindly assists her and a Wicked Witch, who tries to harm her. It is the Good Witch who instructs Dorothy to follow the Yellow Brick Road until she finds the Wizard, for only the Wizard can tell her how to get back home. Continuing on her journey, she meets a scarecrow, a tin man and a cowardly lion. They, too, are searching for what they deem most important to each of them. Together, this unlikely band of comrades journey along the Yellow Brick Road to find the magical Wizard of Oz.

Indeed, this unusual cast of characters exemplify some great lessons for all of us. Dorothy was young and eager for life. But, once she found herself in an adventure, all she really wanted to do was go back HOME! The Good Witch and the Wicked Witch were symbols of the good and evil we encounter along the road of life.

In her travels, Dorothy meets the Scarecrow, tired of being picked on by stray crows as empty-headed and straw-filled. How desperately he wanted to have a brain, so he joined her in the search for the Wizard and a brain. Next, she meets the Tin Man who had no heart! He was too rigid and metallic – constructed and held together only by bolts and nuts. He longed for a heart to FEEL emotion and love. He, too, joined the group to search for the Wizard and to fulfill his dream.

Finally, Dorothy meets the cowardly Lion – so timid, and afraid of everything. He intensely wants to possess the courage to express his noble nature as the mighty "lion" of power and love. He, too, joins in the search for the courage he has always dreamed of.

When they finally find the Wizard, they realize he is NOT really a wizard at all!! He is just an ordinary man, pulling whistles and hiding behind curtains. It was at that moment they realized the Wizard was just like anyone else! It was at that moment they realized that POWER does not come from another person – BUT FROM WITHIN THEIR VERY OWN BEING!

They were searching for what they already had within themselves – their own power! How many of you still walk around like the lost Dorothy, the empty scarecrow, hollow tin man or the timid lion? Do you not realize that the wizard and the power lie always within YOU?

FEAR AND DOUBT

I am sure we all have felt fear and doubt at different times in our lives. Perhaps it behooves us to really look at these states of mind – these attitudes of helplessness and hopelessness.

Fear and doubt are the silent destroyers of life because they give way to despair – the blackest hole of misery ever imagined. Fear and doubt can cloud your common sense and ignite a firestorm of anguish. These negative expressions of human thought and emotion can be deadly!

FEAR is that nebulous, invisible film clouding common sense!

FEAR causes a cold inner paralysis restricting the heart and numbing the brain!

FEAR is a frightening awareness of the vast emptiness between promise and reality!

FEAR hangs on – and on – and on – seeming always to be just around the corner of your delicate, tender thoughts!

DOUBT is that gnawing frustration of skeptical thought that leaves no peace!

DOUBT creates questions that develop a mistrusting corner of pessimism & pain!

DOUBT is that piercing uncertainty that shakes your very foundation!

DOUBT always seems to encourage the endless distrust of others and a lack of faith that weakens your resolve!

Seek the core of truth and cut away from these pools of negative emotion – these worrisome states of mind. They are deadly in their ability to dilute the quality of life.

We did not choose to come back to suffer!

We chose to come back to LIVE – to live a life of joy and goodness.

We chose to come back to right the wrongs of our former misunderstandings.

We chose to come back to cleanse our thoughts and actions – to know that selfishness, greed or lack of compassion is the real death.

We chose to come back because we KNOW deep within our souls, that LIFE is universal and forever; that goodness and righteous living is not just a phrase, but a REALITY WE CREATE!

The seed of that great EYE of the All-Seeing lies within each one of us. Stretch back a little further, and gather your strength as you hurl the disc for the winning record of your good deeds. Gather your determination to free yourself from any distractions of negativity. Conquer those inner demons of fear and doubt. You will find they are really only paper tigers sending illusions to create the false premise of helplessness & hopelessness.

The greatness of the human being lies not in fighting or complaining – not in fear or doubt – but in the astounding capacity to feel Love, to generate Love and TO BE LOVE!

Banish negativity!
Scrub away doubt and numbing fear of the unknown from every cell of your being.
KNOW that your giving heart IS the soul of life.
KNOW that goodness abounds everywhere – within you and around you.
Be grateful, be loving and be kind!

APPRECIATE your worth – your precious goodness and go forth into the Light of understanding and inner freedom!

The great "Being of all Beings", who created this universe, among the many universes and wondrous mysteries of creation, SEES ALL.

Have faith! Build courage! Banish paralyzing fear and crippling doubt!

REFUSE to allow this negativity to assail or cripple you – EVER!!

THE STILT MAN AND STILT WOMAN

The "what if" of distant vision

Have you ever considered "vision from a distance"? I am talking about a "what if" situation.

"What if" you were on stilts, twelve feet high and walked around all day (rather awkwardly), looking at things from a higher, wider perspective?

"What if" everything you saw suddenly looked so small and insignificant in the "scheme of things"?

"What if" the solid, qualities of life – the situations and people who really matter to you come clearer into focus? Would your thoughts be different?

"What if" you suddenly understood the people around you?

"What if" you put the emotions, that really matter to you, into the distant view of your life? Would stilt walking help you see how you have lived? Was it with frantic movement or heavy heart or would you begin to see the immense joy in every little thing that comes your way?

Would stilt walking keep you focused on the violence of things gone haywire, or would the rhythm and order of Mother Nature keep you enthralled with its power and strength?

Perhaps, this vision from a distance could help you gain the balanced view of your life. Or would you feel more removed than ever? Hopefully, this vision from a distance will release the stubborn, myopic views holding you prisoner to the misconceptions and misunderstandings that constantly perplex you.

Yes, it is awkward to move on stilts, and it takes some clever and persistent maneuvering, but the human spirit is very elastic! Just as it takes a lot of patience and skill to mold a lump clay into a handsome statue, what will it take to mold your fluctuating emotions and unsteady thoughts into the beautiful person you truly are deep inside?

Break the mold of artificiality and stubborn misconceptions! Be the person you dream of – for you really ARE deep within – already! You will be surprised at the capabilities you do possess. You will be surprised at the capacity of love and understanding that will pour from the greater part of you. You will be amazed at how people and situations that mattered so dearly to you, that caused much pain and confusion, really do have simple solutions.

Why? Distance...distance is the answer!

It is the distance from "emotional involvement" that will help you to "see" with clearer vision.

It is the distance from emotional involvement that puts back into balance any attachments that cause the strings of your delicate heart (and the endless pool of your fluctuating emotion) to go from freeze-frost to an overwhelming melt.

It is the distance view you need to balance your situations and discover your solutions.

Therefore, go find your mental and emotional stilts and try them on!!

LONELINESS

We must never forget we live in a world of duality. We so need balance. Where there is sorrow, there can be joy. Where there is anger, there can be inner peace. Where there is depression, there can be release. Where there is hopelessness, there can be redemption.

Yes, all these conditions are included under the name of loneliness.

★Why are we so disconnected in this earthly world from finding and being our true, beautiful, spiritual selves?

★Why must loneliness be the mantra of living that destroys our self-confidence and leaves us wanting and gasping for relief?

★Why do we allow the emptiness of life to swallow us into a black envelope of despair?

★Why can't we see so much of the beauty and breathing of life all around us?

There is no simple answer, but there is an answer! We all have problem filled lives. However, we have witnessed a plague, far more deadly than the stealthy viruses and degenerating muscle tissue of aging. It is not a simple one. It is a condition composed of many factors.

I call it the "lack of" –

Indeed, there is a lack of understanding – a lack of belief in self – a lack of hope and wisdom growing – a lack of self-love.

★Are we not worthy of self-love?
★Can we not appreciate the greatness of our individuality – our innate goodness?
★Can we not believe in our own loving nature – our own inner strength?
★Must we so depend on others to fill our life when there is such an abundance of our own inner spirit to move forward?

When can the pain of loneliness die out?
Why must understanding always come from outside of us?
Where is that pool of self-love and appreciation?
Where is that self-admiration and learning for all we have endured?

Yes, we need to share in this life. Yes, we need companionship and loving and a giving of self to another. But, when you feel a "lack of" in life – for whatever reason – do you not realize that you have been working to a glory that is so close to you?

Nothing is elusive. Love continually surrounds you. Get outside of your unstable emotions and hurt rejections. A greater potential is just around the corner!

Believe in yourself! Build the faith in yourself! Build faith in the rhythm of life! Arise each morning with the sunrise and know there is hope and adventure awaiting. Have faith in the goodness of being you! Whatever slight, rejection or rudeness you have felt – with one sweep of enlightenment – know it all can be washed away!

LIVE with the great life force you possess and KNOW deep within your very soul that whatever the rhyme or reason for situations or involvements, or lack thereof, you are still the captain of your destiny – you still are the director of your soul growth. Do not treat it lightly, but treasure all that comes from you and all that is sent to you from that great reservoir of LOVE.

The great gifts you have brought with you (and every human being has them) needs to be understood, realized and appreciated.

Go forth, dear souls – challenge the difficult and create the glory! Loneliness is a condition that can cripple you!

Whatever your path, go forth and know you are not alone, EVER!

YOUR "STOP AND GO" TRAFFIC LIGHTS

There are many types of drivers: young, old, reckless, over cautious, fearful and impatient. There are also angry drivers, reckless drivers, speeding demons, and some with total disregard for the safety of others. Therefore, we have had to institute laws for public safety and policemen to patrol the roads and highways of the land to insure their safety.

Traffic lights were also designed to keep your travel habits in orderly fashion. They assist in making the public roads safe for all drivers and pedestrians. Indeed, traffic lights have become a necessary addition for all drivers to observe. Their green (GO), red (STOP) and yellow (Caution) signals have helped maintain order and safety throughout the land.

Well, you also have astrological built-in traffic signals within each one of you. Did you realize that? Are you paying attention to your planetary cycles and the different aspects that come and go, stimulating your life with opportunities and challenges?

On the highway of your personal life, you need to pay attention to the red lights – the ones that caution you to stop, look and listen to your inner self. Whether you call it a hunch, or the inner voice of conscience, watch your red lights with caution and STOP! Think of what you are doing – only allow that good common sense to dictate your next move. Red is signaling to you that danger is approaching, unseen and unknown. It is that flash of red that screams out – STOP, LOOK and LISTEN to your inner guidance. Some call it a guardian angel that is always with you. Check your current planetary cycles or maybe a difficult aspect that could be cautioning you to be patient and careful.

As you wait diligently for the red light to change, the green light will appear. It will signal the time for you to move – the time for you to sense and seize your opportunity at hand! This astrological green light brings with it the breathing pause of living with ease. Your driving will then be quite smooth as you sail along your own highway of life – confident, and secure.

Then, observe with caution the yellow light that comes next. This is the time that you will need to know a change is coming, but patience and control is necessary. Check your aspects. WAIT! Be Patient! Analyze your strengths and weaknesses.

Your astrological STOP and GO signals are of the utmost importance to you. Treasure them! Use them wisely!

REMEMBERING

Arising from a deep sleep and facing the cold darkness of a winter morning, comforting childhood impressions suddenly appear, in vignettes of early memories.

My riding of a public bus is filled with the memory of a harried mother, entering with her brood of four young children. We all watch her caring look – her intense concern for their welfare, as she sought seats for them. Her young face was clearly lined with weariness and resignation. Yet, here was indicated a love that only mothers understand – a love that left observers inspired with hope for the future.

Walking along the sandy shore of the great expanse of ocean with its calm, rippling waves, we hear the continuing call of the seagulls. We watch as they circle for nourishment. Their sounds and the exhilarating smell of salty air, sends the message that this is a sacred place – a place where we can breathe in the peace and order of nature. Observing the gently tinted blue sky as it blankets the earth, we can suddenly comprehend the awesome beauty of nature and the loving generosity of our Creator.

After a heavy rainstorm, with its deafening thunder and electricity – after the heavy pounding of raindrops and the temporary, powerful cleansing of our polluted atmosphere – the following stillness brings wonder and joy! We stand, transfixed as we watch a rainbow of magnificent color hug the sky. Suddenly, the stillness beckons promise for the future. For a moment or two, the mad whirl of living has stopped. Mother Nature had cleansed the very air we breathe – our life sustaining force – in her faithful duty!

In these gentle memories of the abundance of life – in the constant goodness that surrounds us – surely we must understand the importance of living a life of gratitude. The wonder that abounds, in the most insignificant of places, surely must indicate the enormous love that pours out to us each and every day. Look for your own childhood memories! Do not let them escape and rejoice! Life has its hills and valleys, but through it all, it has its comforts and messages of abundance and love. Every gentle breeze, every budding flower, every quiet moment of reflection and gratefulness brings with it peace and unspoken comfort. Indeed, every brilliant sunrise, alone, fills us with that instant vision of the GREAT LOVE that continually surrounds us!

Never forget to remember –

THE AQUARIAN AGE BEGINS

The Aquarian Age has finally begun! It is now a time where there is greater awareness of individual rights for ALL types of people. Every human being, whether in cities, towns, farmlands, equatorial jungles or lonely islands, will react to the "consciousness" of individual rights and the "desire" to really be free! This is the beginning – where the stirring of the human heart awakens to the call of the inner self – the very spiritual essence of humanity!!

Slavery of all types and forms, be it emotional, political or ideological – will become constantly exposed for the true awakening of humanity. Equality, fraternity and consideration of others are becoming beacons around the world, no longer isolated by distance or strange cultures. Modern electronics binds everyone together in an ever tighter bond of brotherhood. It may seem strange and uncomfortable in the beginning as we witness the vulnerability and closeness of the various countries and cultures. However, as the earth grows smaller, through the widening of communication, the human heart will develop an ever tighter bond of concern for each other.

Yes, the Aquarian Age is moving with rapidity. Some of you are already aware of its influence. For example, if a hand is severed, you will feel the blow. If any child starves, you will weep. If human rights are denied, you will prevail for swift justice! Such is the growing influence of the Aquarian Age – the "Age of Understanding and True Brotherhood". Even those who are not yet aware of this understanding will begin to feel the effects of this New Age. There is a strong awakening everywhere – in your home, your business, your very environment. It happens in your corner drugstore, the local schoolroom and the bustling supermarket just as realistically as on the plains of desert tribes or the steppes of mountain Indians.

The pangs of imminent birth – never easy – are upon us. The NEW AGE is finally beginning its journey as we all move into it with the swift inevitability of changing times, and uneasy, new ways. DO NOT FEAR!! The fear of the unknown lies only in your limited perception. Remember, we all bleed, laugh, cry and soar with the same spiritual essence. This is what the Aquarian Age teaches. This is how the Aquarian Age begins, here and now at this moment of awareness!

At last, the Age of Oneness has arrived, and with it the stirring of the human heart awakening to the call of its sacred self!

It brings the changing of the guard – the evolving spirituality of man to reach the true heights of brotherly love!

Now is the time for the piercing of the teachings of old – the tracings of the great ascended masters! Indeed, the spiritual beginnings are appearing. Your final destiny is at hand to create a world of true gentleness, true peace and brotherly unification.

The energy of these times are powerful – unyielding at times – insistent, demanding and exhilarating. The very earth's atmosphere is changing – attitudes are changing. CHANGE is the watchword! These changes are necessary and sorely needed for this New Age. As it begins its journey, there will be the swift inevitability of changing times and uneasy new ways. Do not fear! The fear of the unknown lies only in your limited perception. As the consciousness of man reaches new heights and soars to unknown possibilities – this will be the time to ask questions – "the how and why we are here"?

There will be much to mislead you and many to misguide you. Keep your own counsel and your own power of thinking and observing. This is the freedom you have earned through countless lives of striving and learning. Now is the time to reap the benefits of all your inner knowledge and intuition. NOW is the time for all men and women to understand the "how" and the "why"?

NOW IS THE TIME! HEAR THE CLARION CALL!

The new world begins with astonishing speed and swift insight. Many of you will begin to see the beyond – the dawning of true human cooperation. The great promised Age of Aquarius has begun! The energies are quickening and the times can be perilous. Although chaos is everywhere, cracking the old boundaries and the misguided philosophies, awake, and look around you – see – feel all about you – within you – within mother earth – the great possibilities finally becoming reality! New planets will be discovered – the great cleansing is beginning and true regeneration is coming at last!

The Age of Aquarius has Begun!

The Brotherhood of mankind stands in the balance.
Hear the clarion call and embrace it with joy!
Now is the time to understand your glorious place in the universe.
Now is the time to realize how intertwined you are with all humanity.
Now is the time to know the importance your small part is to the WHOLE OF HUMANITY!

And to all our future great astrologers – may you grow in wisdom and prosper in true humanitarian love. Blessings are sent to you!

ASTROLOGY
IS THE CONFIRMATION
OF WHAT YOUR "SOUL"
ALREADY KNOWS!

Allow
Your
INTUITION
To
BE
Your
GUIDE!

About the Author

Mary Letorney has been an accomplished English teacher, handling a varied curriculum from English Literature to Drama. She has taught in public as well as private schools. Her drama productions have won both acclaim and recognition in their fields.

Her career in astrology began as a cynical research project. Thoroughly content with raising her family and teaching traditional subjects, she was quite unaware that soon she would be conducting an extensive investigation into the subject of astrology. She has developed practical and unique courses, concentrating on her own method of astrological interpretation and insight. Since then, she has taught and lectured on sound astrological principles; gearing her lectures to be most thought provoking.

Today, her earnest message in this book is a result of her many years as a teacher and astrologer. She simply states: "The Aquarian Age has finally arrived! It deserves to begin with our understanding of that vast storage of wisdom placed in the heavens. The wonder and magnificence of our Universe, with its powerhouse of planetary energies, continually affects us, guides us, and cautions us. Therefore, let us seek to understand our own lives, our precious "free will" and how to try to master our own destiny!"

Other Books Published by Ozark Mountain Publishing, Inc.

Conversations with Nostradamus, Volume I, II, III..........by Dolores Cannon
Jesus and the Essenes..........by Dolores Cannon
They Walked with Jesus..........by Dolores Cannon
Between Death and Life..........by Dolores Cannon
A Soul Remembers Hiroshima..........by Dolores Cannon
Keepers of the Garden..........by Dolores Cannon
The Legend of Starcrash..........by Dolores Cannon
Legacy from the Stars..........by Dolores Cannon
The Custodians..........by Dolores Cannon
The Convoluted Universe - Book One, Book Two..........by Dolores Cannon
Beauty and the Priest..........by Reverend Patrick McNamara
I Have Lived Before..........by Sture Lönnerstrand
The Forgotten Woman..........by Arun & Sunanda Gandhi
Luck Doesn't Happen by Chance..........by Claire Doyle Beland
Mankind - Child of the Stars..........by Max H. Flindt & Otto Binder
The Gnostic Papers..........by John V. Panella
Past Life Memories As A Confederate Soldier..........by James H. Kent
Holiday in Heaven..........by Aron Abrahamsen
Is Jehovah An E.T.?..........by Dorothy Leon
The Ultimate Dictionary of Dream Language..........by Briceida Ryan
The Essenes - Children of the Light..........by Stuart Wilson & Joanna Prentis
Rebirth of the Oracle..........by Justine Alessi & M. E. McMillan
Reincarnation: The View from Eternityby O.T. Bonnett, M.D. & Greg Satre
The Divinity Factor..........by Donald L. Hicks
What I Learned After Medical School..........by O.T. Bonnett, M.D.
Why Healing Happens..........by O.T. Bonnett, M.D.
A Journey Into Being..........by Christine Ramos, RN

For more information about any of the above titles, soon to be released titles, or other items in our catalog, write or visit our website:

PO Box 754
Huntsville, AR 72740
www.ozarkmt.com
1-800-935-0045/479-738-2348 Wholesale Inquiries Welcome